All Are Witnesses

All Are Witnesses

A Collection of Sermons
by Mennonite Brethren Women

Catherine, your words and life have been a gift to me. May you know God's love, grace & power.

Delores Friesen

DELORES FRIESEN, EDITOR

KINDRED
PRODUCTIONS

WINNIPEG, MB CANADA

HILLSBORO, KS USA

Published simultaneously by Kindred Productions, Winnipeg, Manitoba R2L 2E5
and
Kindred Productions, Hillsboro KS 67063

Cover design by Janice Leppke, California
Book design by Fred Koop, Winnipeg
Printed in Canada by The Christian Press, Winnipeg

Canadian Cataloguing in Publication Data

All are witnesses : collection of inspirational
sermons and devotionals / Delores Friesen, editor. —

Includes index.
ISBN: 0-921788-26-6

1. Sermons, English — Women authors. 2. Mennonite
Brethren Church — Sermons.   3. Devotional literature,
English — Women authors.   4. Women — Prayer-books and
devotions— English.   5. Mennonite Brethren Church —
Prayer-books and devotions. I. Friesen, Delores, 1942 -

BX8127.A1A54 1996   252'.097   C96-920094-3

International Standard Book Number: 0-921788-26-6

To

P. Karuna Shri Joel

and all who witness to

What We Have Seen and Heard

of God's Redeeming Love,

Christ's Empowering Grace

and

The Spirit's Reconciling Power

Contents

I
All are witnesses to what we have seen and heard

II
All are witnesses of God's redeeming love

III
All are witnesses of Christ's empowering grace

IV
All are witnesses to the Spirit's reconciling power

Acknowledgments

Thirty-four sermons and seven excerpts from women are found in this collection. Most of these sermons were given in churches primarily to Mennonite Brethren audiences. Many more women submitted sermons, talks, devotionals and meditations. We thank each of them for their courage and willingness to share. Some women submitted only one sermon; others sent seven or eight from which we had to choose. We regret that it was not possible to use more of what was submitted, but perhaps this can inspire others to share their witness both in the spoken and written form.

Marilyn Hudson has been part of this project from the beginning. Her faithful attention to detail and her forthrightness in critiquing, choosing, and planning have been incredible gifts. She has also been responsible for layout and cover design. Rosalyn Thiessen has been more than generous and careful in her copy editing and has contributed many rewarding ideas, including significant work on the themes and organization of the book. The enthusiasm and joy that has been expressed by contributors and participants throughout the process of gathering and editing has deepened my own sense of call and my own desire to continue witnessing to God's love, grace and power.

Cynthia Friesen, graphic design artist for Habitat for Humanity in Americus, Georgia gave us the idea of how to use the cover art to enhance the sectional theme pages.

The artwork chosen for the cover is a sermon in itself. Janice Leppke painted this work in response to Dena Pence Frantz's sermon, "All of Us Are Witnesses." Set in the context of the miracle of the Berlin Wall coming down, perhaps it says better than any of the words herein that God is at work in the world.

No sermon or word of witness is complete without a response. There is ample time and space in this book for you to respond to God's voice, God's call, and God's compassion. Your individual and corporate responses as you study, journal, meditate, discuss, and search the Scriptures "to see whether these things be so" (Acts 17:11) are equally valuable to what is written herein. Please encourage and affirm the authors, yourself and others to continue to develop and use the gifts of life's experiences and your understanding of Scripture to witness to God's love, the grace of Jesus, and the Holy Spirit's power.

Introduction

**All are witnesses
to what we have seen and heard
of God's Redeeming Love,
Christ's Empowering Grace and the
Spirit's Reconciling Power.**

When one's life in one week encompasses a friend's sudden malignancy, an accident that claimed the life of a treasured sixteen year old, the return of a young adult daughter to celebrate and enjoy five other young women with whom she has forged bonds of sisterhood, telephone news of the impending death of a beloved author, who has perhaps taught me more about redemption and reconciliation than anyone else, and a tiny interracial child born to a family who have struggled and triumphed, it is almost impossible not to witness to the grace and power that sustains and blesses.

The sermons in this collection are born out of similar moments of connection and celebration. The preachers and writers have used the Scriptures and their life experiences to share their joy, pain, grief, commitment, insight and vision. Mennonite Brethren women have lived their faith through the centuries from the Anabaptist caves to the steppes of Russia, to the plains of Canada and Kansas, and the cities of Winnipeg, Kinshasa, Fresno, Sao Paulo and Kobe. Like the apostles, "they cannot but speak of what they have seen and heard."

Like Mary Magdalene, the other Mary, Joanna, and Salome, the women who have given their witness in these pages have decided to take seriously Jesus' words, "Do not be afraid; I know you are looking for Jesus who was crucified ... Go, tell his disciples that he is going ahead of you to Galilee, there you will see him." (Matt. 28:5-7; Mark 16:7, Luke 24:8-9) It is not always easy to go and tell, especially when your own eyes are clouded with doubt, fear, or tears. But the sermons in this collection seek to give a faithful witness to what has been seen and heard, lived and experienced. They are shared with the hope that others may come to know Jesus as Lord.

All are witnesses to what we have seen and heard. From the opening of the heavens to the times of waiting, suffering, and dying, there will be glimpses of faith and visions of heaven that will strengthen your own relationship with God and others. Women's preaching has often been characterized as more experiential, more grounded in the everyday living moments of family, work, nurture, and delight. The stories, the history, the flexibility, the waiting, the contentment that stand between the promise and the fulfillment are all here giving witness to what it is like to walk through life with God.

All are witnesses to what we have seen and heard of God's redeeming love. This God is *The Kind of Dad* we come home to. This God journeys with us and sees us when we are in the deserts of our lives. This God births us and loves us like a mother. This God keeps promises and is faithful even when we are unfaithful, forgetful, and sinful.

All are witnesses to what we have seen and heard of Christ's empowering grace. Many of us worry about God's judgment, and our seeming inability to live up to what we've heard, taught, and preached. In the *Parable of the Wheat and Weeds*, one is both comforted and corrected. Freedom, grace, belonging, *Treasures in Clay Pots*, *Living Deeply*, giving thanks *In Spite of the Lions* - these are words and images of empowering grace. And the stories of Mary Magdalene and *Giving Birth to Death in Life* cleanse, strengthen, and purify us to go on living our own stories of grace, empowered by Christ Jesus our Lord.

All are witnesses to what we have seen and heard of the Spirit's reconciling power. All of us experience sin, prejudice, racism, poverty, environmental disasters, conflict, coercive power, and walls that separate and destroy. These are the times when we cry "Maranatha!" and long for peace, hope, and joy. And the Spirit comes to us in restoring a relationship, in rejoicing over walls bridged, walls broken down, and walls with doors. Love, power, forgiveness, restoration, conviction, comfort, shalom — these are the fruits of the Spirit who reconciles, restores, renews, and sends forth.

Mennonite Brethren women have been teaching and preaching from the pulpit, as well as in the classroom, the marketplace and the home. In India, Karuna Shri Joel not only preached, she taught preaching. In Zaire, Mama Kadi and others regularly go on evangelistic tours and preach the word in season and out of season. In Japan, many MB pastors speak freely of how the late Ruth Wiens Funk nurtured them into faith and then taught them to preach, teach, and minister. In Canada and the United States, a few MB women preach on a fairly regular weekly or monthly basis. Many others are given the opportunity to preach only on occasion; or perhaps once or twice a year.

In a few cases the sermon submitted for this collection was simply the first or the last one the contributor preached. Some of the authors have had other sermons published before, in *Christian Ministry*, *Mennonite Brethren Herald*, or *The Christian Leader* but most of these preachers said they had never thought of submitting their sermons for publication. Some of the contributors are more comfortable with pen than pulpit. Some submissions were more suited to spoken word than to written form. It is hard to capture the energy, the spirit, the feelings, the facial expressions, and gestures on paper, but those chosen are clear in their message of love and faith and their witness to grace and reconciliation.

As these sermons are read and reread may they deepen your own experience of God's redeeming love, Christ's empowering grace and the Spirit's reconciling power so that you too may go forth to speak openly of all that you have seen and heard.

Delores Friesen
Fresno, 1996

All are witnesses to what we have seen and heard

JEAN JANZEN

You Will See Heaven Open

John 1:43-51 • I Samuel 3:1-10 • Psalm 139:1-6, 13-18

Our scriptures this morning have given us, once again, the gift of wholeness of life. The calling of Samuel, the awe of the Psalmist, and the miracles of Jesus would seem to be those dazzling interventions in life for which we sometimes long. But these events are, in a sense, dramatizations of what goes on around us and within us every day, what we are called to see, to hear, to taste, smell, and touch.

In writing and teaching poetry writing, I am often reminding myself and my students to use the senses, to be aware of these physical ways in which we know. The tendency is to think and write in abstractions—generalities and ideas often as good and grand as Love and Faith, valuable, and yet often as thin as air, for we listen and know with our bodies as well as our minds, and we find it harder to connect until the language is incarnated, until it becomes flesh. And so these Biblical texts flesh out again—little Samuel rises in his rumpled nightgown, the Psalmist reminds us that we were "knit together in our mother's womb," and Jesus visualizes Nathaniel under a fig tree. Body and spirit brought together, the divine and ordinary in one.

Jesus, in coming to earth, in becoming one with us in the flesh, is our supreme revelation of what this means. The angels descending and ascending are now with us in a new way—the Son of God is here. But truly, angels, the divine among us? Easier to believe on Sunday than on Monday when we rise in the gray of the day to our work, our joints aching. We want it; how can this awareness become more real for us?

One way is to practice it as a discipline, as described in the little book, *Practicing the Presence of God*, by Brother Lawrence. My housewifely spirit responded as he described this discipline in the context of his kitchen work. On the other hand, I didn't have the structure of the monastery around me, the required and possible quiet times, daily communal prayers, or the assistance of that community in my household with my four children. The pietism which my church taught me was a help, and I treasure that stream of dependence on Bible reading and prayer. What needed to happen for me, however, was to move from guilt as the impulse to a freed desire for the presence, and to recognize that no matter whether I sought God or not, God is here. We must simply respond, "I AM HERE." And this we also need to be taught to say, as Samuel was. We think of Samuel as a special child, raised in the temple, but even he thought it was Eli calling. The Psalmist repeats in various metaphors how God's presence is inescapable—no matter how high we fly or how deep we immerse ourselves, God is there. And with Jesus, heaven opened in new ways forever.

So we say, "**SPEAK LORD, I AM LISTENING,**" but it can be terrifying. Samuel discovered that, as did David and the disciples. We want to hear only the words of comfort and reassurance, and what we hear is often wrenching. We hear God's holiness. This is the paradox: the weight and the lightness of heaven coming down to us. This, to me, is the holy challenge of our last decade in this millenium—to allow ourselves to be in the presence. The message of "peace and goodwill" comes with the weight of glory. Not the powdered sugar sifting on our Christmas gingerbread houses, not the fiberglass angel hair, but the blood, pain, and stench of childbirth, first of all, and that happening as we are born again and again. It means the tearing down of walls in our heart, to be willing to go out of ourselves and to really love our family, our friends, even our enemies. "For who can abide the day of his coming?" (Malachi 3:2 KJ).

But heaven come down is also lightness. The angels ascend. It is "Comfort ye my people" (Isaiah 40:1 KJ). It is the promise that we are loved as we are, loved by a holy, awesome God, whom we also call "Daddy." Jesus called us to abide in him, to live in his lap, to know his nurturing and understanding. This is the grace of acceptance and forgiveness which is a deep hunger in us all, one that no human can satisfy. This is the good news. Yet without the weight of God we cannot know his lightness. Without awe we do not really taste the need for mercy. Always it is both, if it is true for us.

When we prepare worship services, direct our choirs, and lead our congregations in singing, prayer, and readings, we ask how we can best awaken our people to God among us. That is why we are here. Nathaniel in the John passage sitting under the fig tree may be somewhat like the person in our pews looking for the comfort of shade, waiting for something to happen, even cynical, perhaps, that any good can come. Then the Presence speaks to them and they are changed.

It is interesting that we don't see Nathaniel's name mentioned again until the end of the gospel, after the resurrection, when again he is waiting among the other bewildered disciples. Their Christ, their leader, has showed himself, has opened his palms, but they are terrified. As disciples, what will be their fate? What are they to do? They wait and are bored, and decide to go fishing. And this time the Presence is a figure dim on the shore, as it sometimes is for us. Dare we follow his instructions? The disciples decide to risk it, and fish on the other side and pull in a full and heavy net. But all this depends on the Presence. And there Jesus is, building a small charcoal fire, blowing his breath for our bodily needs and for our enormous longing to know God. He will eat with his disciples; he will challenge them to follow as he did when he first met them.

Jesus said, "Enter like a child," like Samuel. The Psalmist says, keep that sense of awe and wonder. All of us invite the presence when we respond to life and worship with the freshness of the child, and with the empty feeling in the stomach. The images, music and language of the artist, of the poetry in scripture, of visual symbols, can awaken us. But we must be there. The heavens **are** open and the one who joined with us is here. Such joy and such glory. Thanks be to God.

MARY ANNE ISAAK

Between Promise And Fulfillment

Acts 1 NRSV

Often in our Christian life, the time between a promise and the fulfillment seems to drag on forever. What is the purpose of this time of waiting? If all we do is sit back and wait, the time between the promise and its fulfillment becomes wasted. So what are we supposed to do during that time?

Let's look at the story of Acts 1. There's a promise—the promise of the Holy Spirit—and there is waiting. I used to read this chapter as the necessary introduction to the good news of Acts 2 when the promise is fulfilled and the Holy Spirit is poured out on Jesus' followers. But the story of Acts 1 is itself a message of good news. God's plan is that the time between promise and fulfillment is life-giving; it's a time for learning. The time between the promise and its fulfillment becomes dead time only if it's wasted in impatient, idle waiting.

Let us look at the experience of the disciples. After Jesus' resurrection, he gave the disciples a promise. *"While staying with them, he ordered them not to leave Jerusalem, but to wait there for the promise of the Father. 'This,' he said, 'is what you have heard from me; for John baptized with water, but you will be baptized with the Holy Spirit not many days from now"* (Acts 1:4-5). And in verse

8, the promise is repeated. *"But you will receive power when the Holy Spirit has come upon you; and you will be my witnesses in Jerusalem, in all Judea and Samaria, and to the ends of the earth.'"*

When Jesus promised that the Holy Spirit would come to the disciples, he commanded them to wait in Jerusalem. So they returned to Jerusalem and went to an upper room to wait. But how did they wait? Did they just set up their chairs in a circle and stare at each other? In that case, the waiting would have turned out to be 10 very boring and very useless days.

What kind of response does a promise require? What's wrong with just waiting?

I remember clearly the Christmas Eve when Jon asked me to marry him. After the Christmas holidays he had to drive the 500 long miles back to the town in northern Canada where he was teaching. I stayed in the city. I thought the months till our wedding in July would never end. One day, I was complaining to my married sister. She scolded me, "Mary Anne, don't just keep wishing this time is over. Being engaged is the most exciting time of your life. Marriage is great, but the excitement and the intense feelings of being engaged don't last forever. Enjoy them now. Quit wasting this time by wishing it was over."

Response to a promise is more than just wishing the waiting was over. In Acts 1, the disciples' response to the promise was faithful living. While they waited, the disciples concentrated on following the pattern of faithful living that Jesus had modeled for them. And look at what happened in the disciples' lives while they were waiting. Even before the promise was fulfilled, even before the Holy Spirit was poured out on them, God began changing their lives.

The disciples learned to pray like Jesus prayed. For the ascension, Jesus had taken his followers to the mount called Olivet. This was one place that symbolized Jesus' prayer life. He had been in the habit of going to the Mount of Olives to pray for long periods of time. The last time the disciples had been at this mountain, Jesus asked them to pray with him. Then while Jesus prayed in agony before his betrayal, the disciples fell asleep (Lk. 22:45-46). The mountain reminded the disciples that they were not very good at praying. But now, while they waited for the promise of the Holy Spirit, they gathered together and prayed.

But how were they praying? Verse 14 says that *"All these were constantly devoting themselves to prayer."* The Greek word that describes how the disciples prayed is *homothumadon*. *Homothumadon* is a compound word made of two words meaning to "rush along" and "in unison." It's used only 12 times in the New Testament, and 10 of those 12 are in the Book of Acts. "Rushing along in unison" is a word that helps us understand the uniqueness of the Christian community. Here in the upper room, even before the fulfillment of the promise, the followers of Jesus were rushing along in unison as they worshipped together. They were already becoming a church.

And as they gathered and prayed, they were reading the Scriptures and discerning God's will for their lives. Peter stood up and explained what he understood the Scriptures to be saying to them. They needed to choose a disciple to replace Judas. The group agreed and together they chose Matthias to join the twelve.

Between the time of the promise of the Holy Spirit and the fulfillment, the followers of Jesus responded with faithful living. God blessed them, and even before the promise was fulfilled at Pentecost, God began changing their lives. They learned to talk to God like they never had before. They began experiencing the dynamics of faith, the fellowship and unity of the church, and they discerned God's practical will for their lives.

Then later, when the fulfillment of the promise came, they were ready. When the Holy Spirit was poured out on Jesus' followers, there was an explosion of new power which gave energy to the changes God had already begun in their lives while they waited.

In our lives too, waiting for God to fulfill his promises doesn't mean that we do nothing and wait for God to do it all. Response to a promise means faithful living. And then, even before the promise is completely fulfilled God can do incredible things in and through us.

Last year Jon and I claimed a promise from the Bible for ourselves. We had both been seminary students for four years and were planning to graduate in May. We had many questions about what would happen after graduation. Would we find a job? Where should we apply? And so we claimed a promise from Exodus 33:14. God says to Moses, *"My presence will go with you and I will give you rest."* For us this promise also meant that God would direct us where to go. Then we needed to wait for this promise to be fulfilled.

After much praying, in October, we applied to our mission board. We were accepted for a Bible teaching position in Lesotho. It seemed that God was quickly fulfilling the promise we had claimed. But then we got a letter saying that our mission board was having financial problems and we wouldn't know until March whether we would have a position. March was many months away. Waiting was difficult.

Jon and I waited for a long time for the word from the mission board about whether we would be able to go. It was a time of praying, talking to others, and listening to their words of discernment. While we waited, God continued to be faithful. It became a time of creativity for us. We wondered whether this was God's way of telling us to look for a job in North America, or to apply for ministry with another mission agency. So we explored the possibilities and asked ourselves lots of questions about what direction we wanted our lives to take in the future. In the discussion, we discovered new ideas about our long term goals that we had never considered before. While we waited for God to fulfill the promise we had claimed, God taught us many things. Then in March, the mission board asked us to teach at St. Petersburg Christian University. After much wait-ing, God was fulfilling his promise to direct us. We know that God's presence directed us to St. Petersburg.

In Acts 1, the disciples received the promise of the Holy Spirit. They responded to the promise with faithful living and God came to them during the time of waiting, and made even that time a time of blessing.

What about you? Which promise from the Bible have you been claiming for your own life? Has God begun to fulfill that promise already? Then be glad, and encourage others by telling them how God has been working in your life.

Are you still waiting to see how God will actu-ally fulfill his promise in your life? Then take courage. Waiting for God to fulfill his promises is not just an unfortunate necessity. It's a normal part of God's plan. Despite the confusion and uncertainty, God asks us to respond to his promises with faithful living. And he comes to us during the time of waiting with blessing.

God's plan is that the time between promise and fulfillment is life-giving; it's a time for learn-ing. The waiting is not an idle time of doing nothing; it is a time of growth and creativity, a time when we "rush along in unison" growing closer to God and to each other.

LINDA MATTIES

Facets of Joy:
A Librarian Introduces I John

1 John 1:1-4

In many ways the books of the Bible present a nightmare for librarians. I John does so in more ways than some of the other books. You see, when librarians get a book for their libraries they like to have all the pertinent data right there. There needs to be a title, an author, a publisher, a copyright date and all the other technical details that make the job of cataloguing books a little easier. Unfortunately, in the days when the various books of the Bible were written, neither library science nor the publishing industry had reached their present state of evolution.

Because of this "backward" or "lamentable" state of affairs (speaking , of course, from a librarian's point of view) theologians have written tons of books in which they argue about things like who wrote various books of the Bible, when did the writing occur, what kind of literature is it and what was the specific occasion or problem that prompted the writing.

So, who wrote I John? In some books of the Bible, particularly the epistles, the writer actually identifies himself. Paul tells us who he is when he writes by putting his name at the very beginning. Other biblical writers don't follow his educated example, however, and so the speculation begins.

For many scholars there is a strong belief that someone named John wrote I John. That makes sense to us from our modern point of view. The next question we need to answer is which John or John who? There is more than one John mentioned in the Bible. There is John the Baptist, but he wasn't left with much of a head for literature. We also know that Jesus had a disciple named John.

Unfortunately, John the disciple was only the son of a Galilean fishing magnate and apparently they weren't interested in nor did they have the opportunity for a lot of education. So, if it was John the disciple, when did he enroll in Creative Writing 101? There is one other possibility. They didn't have Dictaphones in those days so maybe he dictated to someone else.

Of course, there are other people who believe that John didn't write the epistle at all. Apparently, it was customary for writers to borrow the names of important and highly regarded people to lend credibility to things they wrote. If this is true, then maybe Phoebe or Nathaniel or Lydia or someone else wrote the book and simply used John's name.

When was I John written? This question goes in two different directions. On the one hand, we want to know the exact "copyright" date or year that it was written. On the other hand, we want to know if it was written before or after the gospel of John. Since we are given no exact copyright date the best we can do is guess. Our guesses are dependent on how we answer the second part of the question. That is, was I John written before or after the gospel?

Those who believe it was written before the gospel find evidence in the gospel that elaborates on the ideas in the epistle. That is, we get more information on the same theme in the gospel with examples from Jesus' life and teaching. Those who believe it was written after the gospel suggest that the ideas expressed in I John assume knowledge of the gospel's existence and of its accepted interpretation.

There are definite references in I John to the fact that the readers had some previous teaching. We don't know, however, if this was written teaching or oral teaching. Remember, this was a time when few people knew how to read.

It was probably written some time in the second half of the first century. Once again, the exact date isn't that important. The message is the same.

What was the setting of I John or where was it written? Again, we are given no clues. There is no specific church or city that is identified in any way. There is some belief that the apostle John lived in or around Ephesus.

What kind of writing or literary genre is I John? On reading the book one senses that the author is addressing a problem that has developed in the Christian community. It has to do with the interpretation and practice of one's beliefs. Some members of the actual Christian community appear to have held some unusual beliefs. In fact, they may have gone so far as to form a splinter group and appear to have been actively attempting to get members from the original church to switch over.

A number of the epistles are responses to specific local problems. However, I John does not appear to be an epistle in the same sense as for example, Ephesians or Romans. There is no salutation to a special group of people and the writer doesn't introduce himself or herself. Instead, it launches right in to make its point. Therefore, it was probably written by someone within the church who was trying to teach the members of the church and help them find their way through the interpretive difficulties that some within the group had been advocating. Many theologians describe this problem as Gnosticism. A modern example of this kind of writing would be if we were to ask members of our leadership team to write study papers on an issue which we as a church are having difficulty with.

Let's summarize what we know so far about I John. It may have been written by someone named John, possibly the disciple of Jesus and son of Zebedee. This same John is supposed to have written the gospel of John, but we're not sure which was written first. The copyright date is probably some time in the last half of the first century. It could have been written in Ephesus or some other part of Asia Minor, which is present day Turkey. It looks like it probably was a study paper written by a church leader to encourage and instruct church members who were struggling with false teaching.

From a librarian's perspective we haven't done too well. Cataloguing this book could prove difficult. However, the one thing we haven't looked at yet is the message itself. Let's do that now.

That which was from the beginning, which we have heard, which we have seen with our eyes, which we have looked at and our hands have touched — this we proclaim concerning the Word of life. The life appeared; we have seen it and testify to it, and we proclaim to you the eternal life, which was with the Father and has appeared to us. We proclaim to you what we have seen and heard, so that you also may have fellowship with us. And our fellowship is with the Father and with his Son, Jesus Christ. We write this to make our joy complete. (I John 1:1-4)

The message is authentic.

The writer begins by setting out the purpose for writing and gives us some "documentation" for the validity of the contents. The writer claims to have the authority of first hand evidence, namely, that which was heard, seen, and touched. The evidence related to the word of life. This word of life had been brought to the community by proclamation and those who proclaimed had first hand knowledge of what they were talking about.

The authenticity of the information is described in a multisensory way. On the one hand, there is a powerful literary device that gives emphasis to the point being made. On the other hand, it denotes real, physical experiences. We are not just getting something third hand. Real ears have heard something. Real eyes have seen something. Real hands have touched something. Real experiences stand behind the message.

The message is about the word of life.

This life is also described as appearing so that it can be seen and verified by witnesses. It is eternal life. The Greek word for "eternal" is related to the English word "eon". The message of this word of life is not just for one generation, but for eons and eons. The gospel of John talks about

Jesus as the word and also as the life. So both these ideas are found in the gospel and in I John.

The message has been around from the beginning.

The first verse starts out with "that which was from the beginning." "That" and "which" are pronouns and if you remember any grammar lessons you know that pronouns have ante-cedents. That means they refer to some noun. So to what noun does "that which" refer? If we only refer to the text in English we might think it refers to "Word" or to "life" or to "father" or to "fellowship" because these are all nouns in that sentence.

However, when we read the text in Greek we discover that the pronoun is neuter. Greek has three genders. None of the nouns in the list fits. "Word" and "father" are masculine. "Life" and "fellowship" are feminine.

To complicate matters even further verses 1 to 3 are all one long sentence. The only neuter reference is the gospel message. The appeal is to the gospel message which they had already heard.

The effect of the message is fellowship

Fellowship refers to meaningful interaction. In order for meaningful interaction to occur there must be some kind of common bond. The common bond is the gospel message about the word of eternal life. Fellowship operates in two directions. There is a "one another" dimension. Fellowship operates between believers. There is a divine dimension. It also operates between believers and God.

The result of the common bond with the message of joy.

The experience of fellowship yields joy. Most of the time, having fellowship is synonymous with having a good time together. This can be just talking about one's week. It can be praying together about one's needs. It can be blending one's voices together in harmonious singing. It can be having a sense of accomplishment from working together.

There are times when we are called upon to fellowship in one another's sufferings. That means standing alongside and weeping with someone who is experiencing a hard time. However, the fellowship mentioned in this particular text is the "good time" variety.

Fellowship around the common bond of the gospel message makes our joy full or complete. The Greek word that is translated as full or complete is related to two English words "plurality" or "plethora." This refers to the many aspects or facets of joy. Just as the many facets of a diamond cause it to sparkle so the many facets of our fellowship give us joy.

The municipality of Matsqui recently celebrated its centennial. Part of that celebration included the publication of a book entitled *The Church in the Valley.*

Somehow, our pastor got wind of the fact that I like history so he gave me the task of writing the history of West Clearbrook Community Church. Since I was a charter member I was qualified to write about what I have seen and heard and touched. I did my best to describe what the church was about. I began with the church's mission statement. I also wrote down some of the things I had seen and heard about as the church tried to put its mission statement into practice.

I would be willing to bet, however, that if someone else had been asked to write the story of West Clearbrook Church, it might have looked and sounded quite different. Another writer may not have referred to the previously written mission statement as his or her starting point. One of the reasons for this is that different people have different interests and concerns. They look at the church from the various angles of these interests and concerns. Another reason is that different audiences require different responses.

If we keep this example in mind, it is a little easier to understand some of the things I have told you about I John. If a church with a four-year history could come up with different versions of its story, it is hardly surprising that interpreting the Bible, which was written thousands of years ago and has been interpreted for just as long, has some difficulties. No wonder interpreters don't agree! It isn't possible to go back and check with the charter members. If they had a mission statement we don't have access to a copy. Nor do we have access to the minutes of their congregational meetings.

All we have is this particular text. It is a text that makes a strong claim to be authentic. It is a text that invites us to join the fellowship of those who have gone before and have accepted its message. We are called upon to stand in solidarity with previous generations of Christians who have heard and seen and experienced the message about the word of life. We are to receive the witness of their testimony so we in turn can pass it on. We, who know what it is to have fellowship with God and with one another, can also be witnesses who see, hear and experience. Our fellowship can know all of the facets or fullness of joy!

DELORES FRIESEN

Baskets of Faith

Exodus 2:1-10 • Acts 9:17-25 • John 6:8-14

Summer's End sermons are a challenge, especially when they are surrounded by farewells and good-byes, leave takings and new beginnings. Our family was up at 4 a.m. yesterday to put one daughter on the plane and will be up again at 4 a.m. tomorrow to see the other daughter off to college. It is an exciting time but also a heart-rending time. Last week, our college students shared some of their adventures of learning and faith, and it was thrilling to see their growth. We also said farewell to one of our pastors last Sunday, and wished this family Godspeed in their new ventures. Saying good-bye is difficult. Some of us try to avoid it; none of us like it. It takes courage and faith to say good-bye, to leave, to risk, to step out into new territory and new ventures. But it is also exhilarating, eye opening, and growth producing to leave, to venture forth, to change venues, jobs, roommates, classrooms.

For some of us, it has been a summer of underemployment and unemployment. For others it has been a summer of health struggles, accidents, dealing with loss of mobility, constant pain and times of confusion and worry, with news of terminal illness and death of loved ones and friends. Meanwhile, around us in the wider context of our community, nation and world, the violence and needs have escalated beyond comprehension—four murders in Fresno in one weekend, doubled car thefts and armed robberies, continued carnage in Bosnia-Herzegovina, escalating threats of war with Saddam, massive starvation in Ethiopia and Somalia, untold devastation from Hurricane Andrew.

It is times like these that test our faith; it is these events and struggles and joys that call forth faith, and cause it to grow. As a Christian, a teacher and a parent, I hear and see my students', my children's, and my own questions and actions, and I wonder, "Will their faith, will my faith carry us through? How firm is the foundation? Can this latest challenge increase faith; or will it threaten to undo us? Will our children and young adults become cynical, bitter, and disillusioned or will they keep the faith?"

In our family, for example, we have just received news of yet another life-threatening cancer, and having lost two friends to cancer only a few weeks after diagnosis this summer does not make it easy to cope with the latest news. We watch our children struggle with these things for the first time and wonder if their baskets of faith will hold.

It is at times like these that I return to the stories of faith—Jochebed and the basket made of bulrushes, Paul let down over the wall in a basket, and the 12 baskets of fragments leftover. The communion table today holds symbols of faith, namely baskets from Bangladesh, Africa, the Philippines, and the USA, strands, colorful, somber, tiny, large, round, square, rough, neat, beautiful, and not so beautiful. The plants in the baskets symbolize growth in faith. Perhaps the colors, shapes, and histories of these symbols can help you remember this teaching from the Word.

I can not imagine what it would be like to make a tiny basket of wet bulrushes, daubing it with bitumen and pitch, knowing for what it would be used. To set an infant, a dearly loved boy child afloat on the Nile River must have taken courage and faith. I will, however, soon know what it is like to set the last child on that journey to college that forever changes their lives—and I suppose the modern tasks of shopping, packing, and reminding are bathed with some similar thoughts and prayers—wondering what will happen to the child, who might discover him, how best to hand the child over to others to care for him, to teach him, to watch over his growth and development. Like baby Moses, our children's safety often depends on the compassion and knowledge of others. The big sister stood by and did her part perfectly; the mother so able to trust, to release, to risk is named in the Hebrews 11 list of heroes of faith; the princess rescued and provided much to develop the needed skills and knowledge for Moses to lead the children of Israel out of Egypt into the Promised Land. But it all started with a basket of faith, a tiny basket, a mighty risk, a life and death gamble and one small child.

Some of you in this congregation know much more than I do about "at risk" children—you live with them, you teach them every day. Those of you who have infants and young children in your care should take courage from this story. A mother's faith, a creative idea, the courage to actually carry out the plan, the ability to allow another to nurture and parent one's child—these are some of the things I see in this first basket of faith. So go ahead and weave your baskets, a daub of pitch here and there, and risk setting them afloat—or if you are the sister or the princess (read adoptive parent, teacher, employer, politician, policy maker, idea person) don't dam up your abilities to see and to make suggestions, don't staunch your urges of compassion! Reach out, see the potential, give freely and generously, ask, keep trying, find a way to give that child or that person what he or she needs. This basket of faith denotes courage, risk, care, compassion and reminds us of the others who mother, father, and mentor our children.

The context of the next story is also a time of danger and opportunity. I asked the reader to begin with verse 17, so you would have the background for when this basket escape actually happened. Perhaps you want to turn to it again—Acts 9. The chapter begins with Saul, still breathing threats and murder against the disciples of the Lord. It then recounts the Damascus Road experience - a remarkable conversion, to say the least. Paul has remained for three days without sight, neither eating nor drinking during that time. Meanwhile Ananias is spoken to in a vision and asked to go to Saul—he questions the sanity of such action, and hesitates to go, but does as he was asked, and Saul receives his sight and is filled with the Holy Spirit. He then was baptized and took food and was strengthened. Quite a faith story! "Miraculous conversion", we would call it, or "a 90 degree turnaround." Faith engendered by visions; a persecutor being stopped blind in his tracks. Surely this kind of conversion is lasting and powerful. Just think of being present at that baptism! For several days Paul stays in Damascus, teaching and proclaiming Jesus, amazing his hearers, and confounding the Jews who lived in Damascus by proving that Jesus was the Christ. But soon there was a Jewish plot to kill him; the gates were being watched day and night, so there was little chance to escape. Imagine yourself in Saddam's Iraq, or war torn Bosnia, or even in Somalia or Ethiopia, or the hurricane's path, without food and water, with a price on your head, within a city surrounded by a wall and gates. Those of you who have been in Israel know these are not ordinary walls and gates. They are 12 feet tall, several feet thick, armed guards at every gate, soldiers and enemies everywhere. There is no place you feel safe, no sure escape from death and devastation—and then you realize what a daring, imaginative escape the disciples of Paul engineered. By night they let him down over the wall, lowering him in a basket. It must have been a good, big, strong basket—the kind they use to carry bushels of grain or loads of produce in the Middle East. Still it took faith, courage, hope, and that willingness again to risk. I wonder if they thought "What if ..... someone sees us?" Or perhaps they wondered if they too, would lose their lives if the escape plot was foiled. Saul the persecutor, becomes Paul the fugitive, running for his life. In a mere basket, he escapes and goes on to Jerusalem, to a fruitful life of three missionary journeys, establishing church after church and authoring a large portion of the New Testament. What if they had not dared to use the basket?

I don't know what your personal walls are or from what you may be running. Perhaps you are bombarded by thoughts or doubts that you can't shake. Or perhaps you fight depression or anxiety, feelings of failure. Maybe you have enemies of the soul or body that seek to do you in. Living with intense or constant emotional or physical pain, weakness, fear, loneliness, rejection or disability takes its toll. Paul's enemies were watching the gates day and night to kill him; but his disciples took him and let him down, lowering him in a basket. I like the community action here—it was a group of disciples that were able to fashion the escape. The story reminds us of the paralyzed man who couldn't get near to Jesus without the help of his friends and a daring rooftop exposure, lowering him down into the room where Jesus was. There are times in our lives when we cannot escape ourselves, our situation, our fears, our enemies, without the help of others. And sometimes it may take being lowered OVER the wall in a basket. Now, I don't know about you but I think it would take faith for me to get in a mere basket and be lowered over one of those massive 12 foot high walls. But the friends provided a way, and Paul made his escape to safety. They took a risk, they did a daring thing, they joined hands to care for their hunted friend. In the counseling room I often experience this basket of faith—somehow in the telling and sharing of difficulties, the pain is lessened, the escape is made possible.

The third story comes from the life of Jesus—and it is a familiar tale. The Sunday School pictures when I was a little girl always showed the young lad with a basket lunch—his five barley loaves and two fish becoming enough to feed all those people seemed only slightly more miraculous to me than the 12 baskets filled with fragments left by those who had eaten. I see the pictures of the children in Somalia, and I think of this story. I hear the teachers' tales and read about the overcrowding, the lack of support and supplies in our schools and I wonder why we seem to always work with scarcity and never with overflow. I sit in on our budget discussions at this church and wonder what would happen if we had $12,000 excess to joyfully distribute instead of a shortfall, or 12 new givers who regularly contributed Sunday after Sunday to the needs of the world and this congregation. I attend meeting after meeting at the seminary which realistically assess the need for students, donors and funds and I wonder will we ever see the 12 baskets full, after all the needs are satisfied?

When there is not only enough to feed the crowd, but there is above and beyond the necessary—when there are leftovers to bless the table, or the day, or the year, or the congregation, then people see the signs of faith, they recognize the Christ, they claim Jesus as indeed the prophet

who is to come into the world! (Jn. 6:14) One lunch, one small basket, blessed—many fed, all satisfied, fragments gathered so nothing may be lost, sign read, message heard, Jesus proclaimed.

When we bring what we have to Jesus and allow him to expand and use what we have in our hands to feed the crowd of competing needs, or the classroom of children, or the world of problems, there is usually enough and many times there are fragments to be gathered and miracles and recognitions to proclaim.

FAITH is made of trust, courage to act, the ability to risk, generosity, the willingness to invest and give one's all. It is in these acts that there is recognition and proclamation of Jesus. When people see the signs of faith, and what is done, they recognize Jesus.

Today I invite and encourage you to: WEAVE! RISK! TRY! GO OVER WALLS! BLESS! FEED! GATHER UP! And may your baskets of faith be increased and strengthened and used! Amen.

• • •

This sermon was preached at a Christian Education appreciation service. The communion table and side shelves had baskets of all sizes and shapes, most with zinnias or green plants, some with fruits and vegetables or pens and note paper. The teachers were invited to take a basket as a token of appreciation for their work in weaving baskets of faith for themselves and others.

SHIRLEY UNRAU

The Pathway of Suffering

Psalm 22, 66:10-12 • Philippians 4:6,7 • II Corinthians 12:8,9

Each of us has our own unique pathway of suffering. Tim Hansel has said, "Pain is inevitable, but misery is optional. We cannot avoid pain, but we can avoid joy. There is no question that life is difficult. In fact, it has been said that God promises four things: Peace, Power, Purpose and Trouble." (*You Gotta Keep Dancin'*. David C. Cook. 1985, p. 15) Elizabeth Elliott defines suffering as "wanting what you don't have or having what you don't want" (quote from address titled *God With Us in Our Pain*).

I want to take you on a journey down four pathways of suffering which I have traveled. As you journey with me, my prayer is that my struggles and victories will encourage you with fresh hope.

Pathway of Disappointment (Psalm 22)

This pathway began in 1961, when I took my two small boys to receive the new polio vaccine. Because I had polio in 1950, I wanted to make sure my sons were protected. I was also encouraged to take the vaccine. That night, I told my husband, "I feel just like I did when I had polio." A fear gripped me at the core of my being. That fear was to be my constant companion and tormentor for many days and months.

I became deathly ill. I lost 20 pounds in one month. The doctors were alarmed, not knowing what was wrong, or what to do. I was hospitalized and went through a series of tests that were almost as bad as the illness.

Eventually I was sent home, sicker than ever. No one knew what my problem was. I was faced with one of life's hardest trials. The battle of the unknown. Waiting, confused and very sick, I felt I was a burden to everyone.

How could this be happening to me? I had given my heart to Jesus. I was his child, but my prayers, my cries to God, my bargaining were all met with silence. MY FAITH WAS SHAKEN. I was a pastor's wife but I didn't know where my God was. I couldn't match my expectations of God to this experience. God had failed me in the test of life, I thought. Yes, my anger with the nurses, doctors, and my husband really sprang from my anger with God. You are not fair, my heart screamed at God. You are hidden. You are silent. And so my confusion and anger raged. I was in a wrestling match with God, but I couldn't win. I was weak in body but weaker yet in soul. I didn't understand God. If God is able to make me better then why doesn't he? I was held captive by a sense of betrayal and abandonment. I was, in reality, disappointed with God. What a dark night of the soul that was.

But where could I go but to the Lord. There were no answers and no comfort apart from him. Sometime, during that long night, I said a weak "YES" to God. Yes to whatever you ask of me. Yes to sickness. Yes to death. Yes to your plan for me. Yes to healing in your time. For the first time since I took that vaccine, peace flooded my soul. The peace of God that passes all understanding was mine. My body relaxed. My soul rested.

God had healed me of the demand to be healed. I decided to rest my case with God and believe the promises of Romans 8:28, " *All things work out for our good, if we love him."* I didn't get better physically for many months. The doctors never found what my problem was, so there was that haunting question, if the illness was emotional rather than physical.

Years later, it was discovered that it was the vaccine that brought about the violent reaction in my body. Very slowly my health returned. And like Job, God showed me that he was a great, good God that I could trust without answers or explanations. The pathway of suffering will have disappointments along the way. It is our choice whether we will face disappointments with God, or disappointments without God.

The Pathway of Peace (Philippians 4: 6,7)

This pathway takes us down a journey that began in 1971. Once again my path became rocky, unknown, and dangerous. Let me paint this picture for you. I, a young mother, now with four children, the youngest just one, am sitting across from the doctor who is saying these words, "Mrs. Unrau, you have the fastest and deadliest of all cancers. This is Tuesday. I want you in the hospital by Thursday for massive surgery that will take over six hours. I don't know if I can do anything for you. I will do my best." Then he left us.

By now, I had walked with my God a much longer time. I had proven that he was faithful. I must tell you, this time, to the glory of God, there was no anger, no fighting, no demands. There was the sweet rest in the pillow of God's love that can never be explained in human words.

God blessed me with the joy of his presence and the comfort of his word. I Corinthians 6:19 - 20 became a special life line for me. *"Don't you know that your body is the temple of the Holy Spirit, and that you are not your own. For you have been bought with a price: therefore glorify God in your body."* I decided to trust God to look after his property - my body. The surgery was extensive. The malignancy had traveled from the calf of the leg to the groin. For 10 days the doctor thought the leg would have to be amputated. The reality of pain and suffering was all there but the peace and rest of soul flowed over my life. Five years ago the cancer returned. One specialist told me I was living with a sleeping giant. "No, " I said, "I'm living with a loving God."

Over the years of walking with God, trusting him in small and large crisis, I have built up what I call "a train load of trust" in God. That train begins with the locomotive of faith and trust in Jesus Christ as our personal Lord and Savior and then throughout life we have the opportunity to build on that train, car after box car of trust and confidence in God. The longer that trainload gets, the more power it has to pull us through the steep and rough places along the pathway of suffering.

The Pathway of Relational Pain (Psalm 66:10-12)

This pathway takes you to a depth of suffering that is more difficult than physical pain.

Nothing hurts like a friendship or a marriage that is shattered. There was a time when we could say we had lived at peace with all. (Romans 12:18) Yes, there had been conflicts and turmoil both in our home and in our churches, but we had always been able to work them through to a successful conclusion. And then we became involved in a situation in a church where we could not make peace, regardless of how hard we tried. For the first time in our lives, we had an enemy, one who would not look at us or speak to us for almost two years.

Swindoll says, "to be ignored is more painful than to be slandered." ("Insight for Living" quote) The issue was peripheral - the pain unmatched. We knew what it was to be shunned, falsely accused, no course of appeal, no response to our pleas. We had to rest our case with God and let him be the judge and avenger.

The Pathway of Thorns (II Cor. 12:8,9)

One of the more difficult aspects of the pathway of suffering is the thorns along the way. Thorns will not kill you but they are a constant source of irritation that can wear you down and cause you to despair. Your thorn may be constant headaches, back pain, insomnia, allergies, a difficult spouse or no spouse, a rebellious child or life in a wheelchair. Whatever your thorn, it remains a constant challenge to be bitter or better. Paul had a thorn. I'm glad we don't know what Paul's thorn was. That way we can all identify. One thing we do know is that he asked three times for it to be removed and God said "No" to one of the greatest Christians of all time.

Moses too received an emphatic "No" to his pleading prayer to God. (Deut. 3:23-29) God actually had to reprimand Moses, his faithful servant as he told him, "That is enough, do not

speak to me anymore about the matter." The answer was "no" and that was final.

Jesus, our prime example, asked God the Father three times to remove the cup of suffering from Him. (Matt. 26: 36-48) The Father denied that agonizing request of his son, Jesus. On the cross Jesus cried out, "My God, why have you forsaken me?" (Matt. 27:46) Jesus too experienced the denial of his prayer, the agony of suffering and the "why" of God's way. God was silent in the time of his deepest pain. In all of his suffering, Jesus' greatest prayer was that God's will would be accomplished in his life, in his suffering and in his death. His suffering "worked out for the good" of our redemption.

What Do We Do When God Says "No"? What Life-Changing Principles Can Help Me Face My Suffering?

1. *Run to the Word*
Let the word of God become your source of comfort, strength and joy. Often, in times of trial, the only thing I could do was run to the word of God for comfort and perspective. Never has God's word failed me.
2. *Be Honest With God*
a) Honesty involves a consistent prayer life. We are told always to pray and not give up (I Th. 5:17) and to come boldly to God's throne, to find help in time of need (Heb. 4:16). The Bible says in James 4:2 *"often we do not have what we desire because we do not ask of God."* Prayer is not demanding of God, or telling him what to do; it is lining oneself with the will of God, in obedience to the word of God (Eph. 6:18).

At times we have prayed alone, often with each other, and asked others to pray with us. Occasionally we have fasted and prayed not to twist the arm of God, but to do everything we can to be obedient to scripture. We have followed the commands of Luke 8, and have sought to be persistent in prayer until God gives us his answer, Yes or No!!

Learning to be honest with God and honest with yourself is important. Admit the pain, go below the surface. Being real brings health to the emotions. Covering up feelings causes greater distress. It was safe for Job to be real and honest and it is safe for you.

b) Honestly accept the mysteries and confusions of life. Don't try to have all the answers to life's sufferings. They are just not there. We want control in life, and God gives us confusion. We want mastery and God gives us mystery. Why? Because **we're not home yet!!!**

3. *Write Out Your Thoughts*

Times of suffering are often times of confusion. Writing down your fears, your questions, your resolve to trust God will help you settle your mind and clarify your thoughts. There is great therapy in talking and writing out your grief to others and to God. A spiritual journal has been a great source of comfort and release to me. The Psalmist David often embraced this source of expression and through writing worked through his pain. Swindoll has said, " Thoughts disentangle themselves over the lips and through the fingertips." ("Insight for Living" quote)

4. *Cultivate a Thankful Spirit*

Learn to focus on your blessings and count them. Naming your blessings and thanking God for them continues to make them primary thoughts. The more you repeat something, the more real it becomes. Habakkuk 3:17-19 is a wonderful example of how to cultivate a thankful spirit.

Habakkuk envisions a worst case scenario. He pictures a total crop failure with no figs, no grapes, no olives, no food, no sheep and no cattle. That would spell disaster for any farmer, but Habakkuk's resolve is this: *"Though there is failure on every front, yet I will rejoice in God my Savior. The Sovereign Lord is my strength."* This is joy and thanksgiving at its best with circumstances at their worst. We too, can choose to trust God.

Sing the Songs of the Lord along the pathway of suffering. I can't tell you the source of comfort and joy this had been in my life. Songs I have memorized in time past have become alive to me during times of trial. Many times along recent paths of suffering song has lifted my heart to God. Sing the songs of the Lord - it will make you thankful.

5. *Let Others Inside*

God has placed you in a family and in a church body so others may bear your burdens with you (Gal. 6:2). Don't be too proud to admit a need, come forward for prayer or ask others to pray for you and help carry the load. Call for the elders in obedience to James 5: 14-16. One of the greatest blessings of my extended stay in the hospital for 23 days was to see how the family of God rose up to bless our family in every possible way. Imagine my husband home alone with four small children. What a joy to see the body at work. What a comfort to know that not only are people praying for you and lifting you up to the father, they are also sharing practical help.

Let me warn you though, when you let others inside you may discover as Job did that some of your friends may disappoint you. One woman sat by my bed, wept and said, "Why are you here, you have done nothing wrong, it should be me." Another asked in hushed tones, "How long does the doctor give you?" Another one wrote me a letter of attack and said. "I can't believe you are saying God is being glorified in your sickness.

Don't be so proud. Ask those who have faith to pray for total healing and then God will be glorified." I was devastated. I felt that person was trespassing on private property. How could she know my heart, or my relationship with God? It is a very sacred trust to be allowed to walk through the door of another's suffering. We must be careful to respect the sanctity of that person's struggles.

6. *Make Knowing God Your Goal*

Let the path of suffering lead you to a deeper knowledge and love of God. Make your goal in life to **get to know God better**. This is the only goal in life that no one can block.

The more we make our goal in life getting to know God better through every circumstance of life the more we will view suffering as something to be glad for, because the end result is being more and more conformed to the image of Christ. As you make your number one goal in life to get to know Jesus better, then he will be your dearest friend, walking with you, before you and sometimes carrying you along the pathway of suffering, to victory in suffering and ultimate release from suffering.

May our deepest desire be to hear him say, "Well done, my child, enter into the joy of the Lord!"

LORRAINE DICK

Known by God

Psalm 139

Psalm 139 is a prayer. Most of this psalm is spoken to God about God. The writer of this psalm confesses with words his understanding of an all-knowing God. How much God knows and how little we know!

To be known by God ... Is it safe to say that all of us have a feeling or some kind of a knowing that God knows? I think so. But my desire to control my own life does not always like the fact that God knows. I try to liken my relationship to God in human terms. To a greater or lesser degree, I can determine what I want you to know about me. I can control the information I give you about my personal life or my thoughts. I cannot control what you think about me, but I can try to control what you know about me (barring rumors).

My relationship with God cannot be thought of in human terms. This is a supernatural relationship. There is no hiding from his knowing all about me; there is no covering up his knowing.

O Lord, you have searched me and you know me.

So, Lord, you know me! What does it mean that you know me, Lord? My dictionary tells me that it means to be familiar or acquainted with, to have an understanding, to be informed, to have a perception of.

Sometimes that feels very comfortable. I'm glad that you know me. I'm glad that you have searched me, that you have looked deep into my heart. It's your loving concern about my life that causes you to know me. Some days, it's just very hard to talk about what is deep in my heart.

On the other hand - there are days when I don't want you to know me at all. Those are generally the days I've chosen to say or do something that I am quite sure is not in keeping with your ways. Those are the days I want to control the outcomes in my life.

I need your knowing those days too - the probing of why I have chosen to walk on my own or away from you.

And it's not only that you know me as a casual acquaintance, you have searched me out. You have investigated my being. Your search has been for a person like me with my character qualities, with my abilities and gifts. You completely understand my intentions, my attitudes, my secrets, my peculiarities, my foibles, my humor and my pensiveness. Yours, Lord, isn't a knowledge of discovery knowing, but a knowledge of complete understanding of me. You invite me to discover you.

You know when I sit and when I rise:

You really do know about me, don't you? Let's start with the sitting and the standing. I sit in such variety of positions and places. I sit at work, I sit at home. I sit when I'm on my way to work. I sit with friends, I sit at meal times. I sit to read, to watch TV. I sit to relax, I sit when there is nothing else to do. I sit impatiently, I sit with resignation, I sit uncomfortably. In all of those 'sit'uations you know me.

Then I rise - I get up to go away from where I have been sitting. You know about that as well. You see my rising from my bed in the morning. You know whether I am a morning person or not. Do you ever smile at the half-closed eyes of those of us who struggle to get going? Do you laugh at the eagerness with which some of us jump up to meet the day? Does it please you to see that even in the morning you have created us to be unique?

Or when I rise to meet people, rise to participate in an activity, rise to move about - all of that rising you know about. It doesn't matter to you whether I'm in rest or activity - you love me and care about me.

You perceive my thoughts from afar.

I was thinking, Lord, that ...

But you already know those thoughts don't you? Mostly my mind is not too still. How quickly I move from one thought to the next. As soon as I wake up, I begin active thinking. What will this day hold? Oh yes, I have to do that assignment - I wasn't really looking forward to that. Or, wow, Lord, today's the day!

All the plans I think out, the imaginary conversation I'll have, the writing I'm going to do - all are thoughts that are not strangers to you. Sometimes my thoughts and plans are dashed with one stroke of the pen or one ring of the phone. You know how hard or easily I do that.

You know the thoughts that I have about my family. You know the pressures, you know the good days and the bad. You know the thoughts I have about my co-workers. And yes, you know the new creative, exciting thoughts that give enjoyment to my day.

Oh yes, I almost forgot. You also know the impatient thoughts I have about the slow driver in front of me as I leave to go home. Ah, Lord God, all those thoughts - you see them as they begin to form, as they come to the front of my mind, as I chose what to do with them.

You discern my going out and my lying down:

Going out? Where, Lord? Well, I guess it's the daily going about with my life tasks. It's also going to find new ideas, going to search for new things, going to find what was left behind. You understand how I pursue my life. You know the secret places of my mind (where I go to fantasize). You know the secret places I visit (where I go to escape). My going out can be positive or negative. God knows.

And when it's time to lie down at the end of the day you are there with me. Lord, sometimes I relive the day - the decisions I made, the conversations I had. I replay and try to analyze what happened, how it went. Every now and then I wish I could do things over again. But I can't and so eventually I have to leave my actions with you. Lying down - you know when I need rest from the task of parenting or work or life in general.

You are familiar with all my ways.

Searched and known. You understand my unique ways - the things that make me, me. In fact, like our individual fingerprints you have given me a personality just as unique. Familiarity with my way means that you are well - acquainted with how I order my life. You see the routine, the ordinary and mundane and understand my reactions. You also know the extraordinary and uncustomary things that keep my life on the edge.

Lord, thank you for your familiarity with me. How wonderful to be known and accepted. How freeing to approach you to continue your work in my life.

Before a word is on my tongue you know it completely, O Lord.

Words - what power can come out of the spoken things I say. With words I can encourage someone, break another's spirit, cause an acquaintance to draw towards me or send a sibling running for cover because of my harshness.

"Sticks and stones may break my bones, but words will never hurt me." That childish saying just isn't true. Words heal, hurt, build up, tear down, cause a smile, cause a tear.

And all of these words are known by you. Not one word passes my lips, but you know what I will say. Thousands of words pass my lips each day and God knows them all. Mostly, Lord, I don't think about your knowing my every word.

I think about the words I have used that have intended to hurt. I stop now to acknowledge my thoughtlessness and selfishness in using those words. God, forgive me. But I also think about the words that have brought joy and healing.

Quickly I want to praise you for those words as part of my life. O Lord, you are invited to be the gatekeeper of my mouth.

You hem me in - behind and before;

"Hemmed in" - my first thought, I admit is, What?! Confined, hedged in? Let me out! God, haven't you given me a free will to respond to life? I want to make up my own mind and not be restricted by constraints. That's my individualism responding.

However, if I take some time to think about this hemming in as something that is a protection - then it becomes a comfort. God behind me. God before me. That means that God knows all about my circumstances, all about my history and all about what is yet to come. Hemmed in I can trust him to show me his loving care and understanding.

I am under his scrutiny - under his close analysis and inspection. It's as if your hands are cupped around my life. No matter which direction I look - I find God is there. Whether I have lived for him or not, he is there.

you have laid your hand upon me.

Thank you for the blessing that you provide for my life. You have placed yourself around me as well as covered me with your blessing. I remember the times in my life when hands have been laid on me in prayer. I feel so privileged to be prayed for - for service, for healing, for blessing. And just think, God, your hand is always on me.

Such knowledge is too wonderful for me, too lofty for me to attain.

Heavenly Father, I stand in awe and wonder at you and what you do in my life. You know me! This knowledge you have of me eludes me, it escapes me. I don't have the capacity to understand or fathom that you know me that completely. I don't know myself like that.

In that case, Lord, if you know me so well, why am I so slow to talk to you about my life situations? Why does it take me so long to acknowledge my need of you? Why am I afraid to be honest with you? You don't only know - you can give me the knowledge of following your ways and doing what's best for my life.

At the end of this chapter, the voice turns personal and prayerful. While the psalmist has acknowledged God's knowledge he now turns toward God and invites God to do what God does best - knowing us.

We can acknowledge that God knows us , but God still waits to be invited into our lives. With this invitation, God comes in to lovingly and carefully help us work out what our lives should be like.

As you think about your own relationship to God, I invite you to pray with me the prayer found in the last two verses of this chapter, if you are willing for God to know you.

Search me, O God, and know my heart
Test me and know my anxious thoughts.
See if there is any offensive way in me,
And lead me in the way everlasting.

IRMA EPP

"When the Joyful Harp is Silent . . ."

Psalm 30

I wish you could have met my mother. What made her "special" was that in spite of her busy schedule, she always took time for her own family. And while she moved about she frequently sang one of her favorite songs: "Marvelous Grace of our Loving Lord." She especially liked the fourth verse:

Marvelous, infinite, matchless grace,
Freely bestowed on all who believe;
You that are longing to see His face,
Will you this moment His grace receive?
Grace, Grace, God's grace, ...
Grace that is greater than all our sin.

Until last year, her phone calls were fairly frequent. Now her calls and songs have ceased. She frequently sits in her worn sofa chair in the corner of her room at Sunset Manor in Clearbrook and weeps. She doesn't remember the happy times in her life; she often doesn't remember our names, nor what day in the week it is. When I went to see her just before Easter I, too, sat and wept. This was not the mother I once knew, the one who had nurtured me.

I don't know what you do when difficulties come your way, but when I have to face difficult situations in my life I frequently turn to the Psalms or the Book of Job. Somehow, these Scriptures express what I'm feeling; they speak about things that matter most at that particular point in time. These passages allow me to express my disappointments with God, my doubts, my frustrations, even my suppressed anger when things go awry, out of joint, out of sync.

But for many people this is uncomfortable, even threatening. I know it was for me. I had been taught that a 'true' Christian should move from victory to victory, from strength to strength - always on top of things, always in control regardless of the circumstances.

But this is a romantic, unrealistic view of spirituality. Bruggemann, in his book *The Message of the Psalms* (1994) states that there is an untamed darkness present in our lives that needs to be acknowledged. We cannot obtain new life, new insights, new light until we acknowledge that.

Our first reaction when difficulties come our way is to pretend they are not there. We want to be positive, we want to speak about our successes. We don't want to raise disturbing questions. But certain passages including the Psalms and the Book of Job, encourage us to face our darkness. It's amazing what can happen when we dare to do that.

Using Psalm 30 as a base, we want to look at a few of these passages. They are called Psalms or Songs of Lament. These songs of lament are not neat little packages tied together with pretty bows. They are often ragged on the edges. Neither are they necessarily written in chronological order. They reflect the writer's state of mind whose ordered world is unraveling at the seams. Yet, in spite of this, there is a certain pattern that emerges - a certain flow or movement that occurs within these psalms. I got very excited when I suddenly realized that these patterns reflected my own experience.

In Psalm 30, King David tells his story of experiencing and coming through some deep trouble. Let's begin with verses 6 & 7:

> When I felt secure, I said, "I will never be shaken." O Lord, when you favored me, you made my mountain stand firm.

Eugene Peterson's paraphrase reads:

> When things were going great I crowed, "I got it made. I'm Yahweh's favorite. He made me king of the mountain."

These verses begin with a description of how things were before the difficulties came. Life was good, life was generous; it was predictable - a description of a season of well-being. And with it came a feeling of security, a sense of being in control. *"I will never be shaken, I have got it made!"* (v. 6). And underneath was an assumption that things would always continue like this.

But then, something happened; that firm mountain began to tremble and shake. *"But when you hid your face, I was dismayed"* (v. 7). The para-

phrase reads: *"Then you looked the other way and I fell to pieces."* A shift took place in David's life, a shift from an ordered life to one of disarray. From the text it can be assumed that David came down with a grave, life-threatening illness. Whatever the problem was, it shattered him, "This can't be happening to me! Bad things should not be happening to Yahweh's favorites."

What is David's first response? *"To you, O Lord, I called; to the Lord I cried for mercy"* (v. 8). To the Lord he addresses the cry of his heart. It's the cry that he shares with his closest most understanding friend. He knows that he can come into the presence of God bringing nothing more than a cry for help.

Often this cry in the Psalms seems overstated. The speaker wants to make a point; he wants God to act now - quickly! In one of David's other songs of lament, Psalm 69:1-2 , he cries:

> Save me, O God, for the waters have come up to my neck. I sink in the miry depths, where there is no foothold.

This may be an exaggeration, but it is a vivid description of how we feel when disaster strikes and our world crumbles.

Frequently in their complaints, the speakers of the Lament Psalms seem to hold God accountable for the present situation. "But when you looked the other way I fell to pieces."
". . . when you hid your face, I was dismayed" (Ps. 30:7b). Whose problem is it? Yours, Lord. It's almost as if the speaker is suggesting that because of God's lack of attention, this trouble has arisen. Therefore, God should make it right - it is God's responsibility to look after it.

The speaker goes even further. He begins to bargain with God. He gives reasons why God should act now. In verse 9 he lays his case before the Lord.

> *What gain is there in my destruction, in my going down into the pit? Will the dust praise you? Will it proclaim your faithfulness?*

The Peterson paraphrase reads,

> *Can you sell me for a profit when I'm dead? auction me off at a cemetery yard sale? When I'm 'dust to dust' my songs and stories of you won't sell. So listen! and be kind! Help me out of this!*

What David is saying is that if he's dead he won't be able to sing his songs of deliverance and praise to God anymore. God would not really want that, would he?

Sometimes this kind of candor is almost shocking. We can talk to God like this? Say it as it really is? The Psalmist recognizes that the speaker must be permitted to speak the unspeakable before God. Who has not felt cheated when disease or illness strikes, when you see the pain of disorientation in your mother, when you walk through the pain and separation of death, or when you prayerfully hand in one resume after the other and you are still unemployed after six months? Out of these depths of struggle and pain we are permitted to ask God some hard, tough questions and to bargain. In times like these nothing is out of bounds. We know God is present in our darkness. If we didn't believe that, we would not be addressing him in the first place. Expressing what we are experiencing helps us to acknowledge our situation. It forces us to face reality.

Once we have done that, something happens.

We can't explain it. Suddenly there is a shift from desperation to joy, from petition to praise. In Psalm 30 it happens between verses 10 and 11. The darkness in the soul of the speaker has been lifted. It almost seems as if a resurrection has occurred.

The speaker has been changed through the process. By daring to be honest with God something has happened in their relationship. It's as if he has been given some new insights, as if he has received a new set of glasses that can see farther and deeper than the ones worn before the trouble began. Look at the new insight the Psalmist shares in verse 5.

> *[God's] anger lasts only a moment, but his favor lasts a lifetime; weeping may remain for a night, but rejoicing comes in the morning.*

After this shift happens, the speaker, filled with wonder, breaks out in these ecstatic expressions of praise in verses 11 and 12.

> *You turned my wailing into dancing; you removed my sackcloth and clothed me with joy, that my heart may sing to you and not be silent. O Lord my God, I will give you thanks forever.*

Not only does he praise God, but he invites the congregation to praise God with him. *"Sing to the Lord, you saints of his; praise his holy name"* (v. 4).

Praise of this nature usually comes after a person has walked through a problem that seemed unresolvable. The situation may not necessarily have changed; sometimes it does, sometimes it doesn't, but you, the person walking through it, have changed. Human life is never static. It consists of different seasons. We must experience the harshness of winter before we can experience the surge of new life in spring. It is out of these experiences that trust and confidence are born. The Psalmist illustrates this very graphically in Psalm 126:6:

> *[Those] who go out weeping, carrying seed to sow, will return with songs of joy, carrying sheaves with [them].*

How is all of this being carried out in the situation with my mother? I'm still in process, but a close friend who realized I was mourning the situation gave me a wonderful article to read.

When I read it, I heard my mother speaking:

I would ask you not to think of me as absent or gone, but as present and disabled. Because I might not know who I am I need you to tell me who I am . . . you would honor me by telling me the highlights of my own pilgrimage. Did I do something well? Did I make a difference? Did I enjoy some victory worth mentioning to your children? (Gary Hardaway. "Father Pens Open letter to Grown Children About his Twilight Years". *Fresno Bee*. July 23, 1994)

It's amazing what is happening. In the remembering and telling I am discovering joy, ...deep joy and gratitude for the legacy my mother left me.

JOANNE KLASSEN

Tell Me the One About . . . ?

Joshua 4

There is a story that my parents tell about me as a child concerning my favorite book *How Does Your Garden Grow?* Apparently I asked to have it read to me so often I had it memorized, could recite it, and could tell when I was getting the abbreviated version.

The Bible is filled with stories of people: some who were successful and powerful, but many who were discouraged, felt weak, had difficult relationships, failed more than once and experienced hardship. In spite of our Bible being filled with people's stories, we call it "God's word." It is God's word because we read of people who experienced God in ordinary, surprising and miraculous ways. The way we discover God, in the Bible, is by reading about how God was made known to people, whatever their circumstance.

The story in Joshua 4 is important because it emphasizes the primary way we learn about God —through people, in dialogue, stories, and the endless interpretations of stories. In Joshua 4 the people of Israel learned to know God in a special way through Yahweh's miracle at the Jordan. Yet the story itself seems to be a weaving together of several versions of the same story. Just as Joshua 4 is a blend of different accounts of the same

story, so each of us, as a child of God, has an important version of the story of how we have come, and are coming to know God.

The stories of God's people serve to reveal God and God's work in people's lives. As these stories are lived, remembered and reflected upon, they influence the future. God's self-revelation comes through stories of the past, and these stories affect both the present and the future.

Revelation through stories of the past

When I was about sixteen I interviewed my grandma. The story that had the greatest impact on me was one about how she stopped singing when grandpa died. She didn't sing for years and years out of grief, and then when she was finally ready to sing again, the years of disuse had affected her voice. That story shook me up. How could anything stop someone from singing?!! I thought that the worse my grief the more I would sing, even if the songs were mournful and solemn.

Through the stories of my grandmother I have revisited my family history many times, though I confess I still don't know as much as I would like. The lives, words and attitudes passed on to me have been models to me, have brought me insight into my own self, have caused sorrow and have cultivated empathy.

In chapter 4 of Joshua, the stories to be told are also from the past. There are two dynamics about stories of the past that I'd like to examine.

The first is about human development, or life changes. The stories I have shared this morning were told to me at critical moments in my development—*How Does Your Garden Grow?* was in my first two years, and my grandmother's stories were in mid-adolescence. Both of these stages were times of intense questioning, exploration, and self-discovery. The stories link me with the past, for better or worse, and are part of my identity. In chapter 4 the instructions to Israel are "when your children ask. . ."and "when your descendants ask. . ." (vv. 6 & 21). The story implies there are significant teachable moments in family living and the children are to ask the questions in order to receive the answers. Let's look at how these relate to our experience of the church as a family.

Local churches can be both parent and child. Within the church there are persons with years of faith experience and faithful living and others with shorter faith stories, either because of younger years or more recent experiences in coming to faith. This is one of the delights and challenges of being God's people—we are diverse in the life stages we bring to worship, learning, congregational meetings and programs.

As a church, how do we handle our developmental stages? Do we encourage questions? Do we listen to the stories that will guide us? When we are torn between running into uncharted territory and changing at a slower pace, how do we handle the discomfort that rises among us? For us right now there are some issues—some among us feel we are discarding too much of tradition

and not heeding its wisdom on topics as diverse as lifestyle, music or belief. Some among us feel we can't change fast enough—they have a vision for the church and press us to continue running at a great speed. There is a tension among us, largely unnamed and unrecognized, though certainly felt. This is an important developmental phase for the church. We cannot simply rush through it in order to dispense with our feelings of discomfort. Nor can we deny the presence of those feelings in the hopes they will disappear. We cannot run from them, laying blame at other peoples' or groups' feet, or by becoming expert at small talk. Instead we must acknowledge our feelings of uncertainty, discomfort, frustration, anger or alienation. We must hear our sisters and brothers when they ask questions or tell stories. We must remain open to one another.

The second dynamic about the past in our text comes from a Hebrew word, which is translated "know" or "tell" in most of our English translations. It means to "know by experience." In the stories of the crossing of the Jordan it appears with this meaning four times in chapters 3 and 4.

Joshua 4: 21-22 reads, *"when your descendants ask. . . 'what do these stones mean?' tell them. . ."* and verse 24 reads, *"He did this so that all the peoples of the earth might know that the hand of the Lord is powerful. . ."*

In Hebrew these words imply an "experiential knowing, a knowing with both head and heart at one and the same time." (Martin Woudstra. *The Book of Joshua*. Eerdmans. 1981, p.95) It is vital to realize that these significant stories from the past can be communicated in a way that fosters this "experiential knowing."

Knowing by experience unites the split we often make between thinking and feeling, or learning and doing. Our faith story needs to be passed on through all the senses: our ears receive knowledge through sermons, classroom lectures, choral singing and many other things we hear. Our ears pass on our faith when we listen to a child before asking him or her to do something; or when we hear another person's story. Our eyes experience knowledge when we lie on our backs and watch the northern lights on a cool fall night. Our eyes pass on experiential knowledge when we meet a grieving person's eyes with empathy. Our hands receive knowledge of love when a parent strokes our hair, and we pass it along when we give new and used items to a neighbor, friend, or stranger who needs them. We taste the story of faith in Communion when we eat the bread and drink the cup. We pass on the story at potlucks and housewarmings.

The two uses of this Hebrew word are in verses where the context is knowledge and experience of God. In Joshua 4 that knowledge comes through the miracle at the Jordan and the stones which are a memorial to that event. On the one hand, the crossing of the Jordan was miraculous and special. On the other hand, the stones were exceedingly ordinary and not arranged particularly artistically. In our journeys, knowledge may come through a miraculous healing or an ordinary Sunday School lesson, but we are drawn to the source through both.

Some people have found possible "scientific" or "natural" explanations for the parting of the Jordan's waters, but if we think the focus of the whole story was to give scientific proof that the ark of the covenant stopped the water so the Israelites could cross, we would be missing the point. The point is that the stones are a sign of the miracle, which is a sign pointing us to God. This experiential knowledge is knowledge of God

in us and through us, around us and beyond us. How is God being revealed to you? What are the signs pointing you to God?

Revelation in the effects of story on the present

Experiencing the stories of the past influences our encounters in the present. There are two main categories of people in this story: the askers and the tellers. The tellers may be experiencing a sense of *deja vu* because this story is very similar to the Exodus account of the Israelites' escape when God parted the waters of the Red Sea. The similarities are striking, but there are some differences. For instance, a whole generation has passed since the Exodus. There is a different leader, Joshua, instead of Moses, and the Israelites are not being pursued by Egyptians.

The similarities are also significant. Our passage says these events took place on the tenth day of the first month—the same day the Passover lamb was to be selected to commemorate the rescue from Egypt. Also, the rod held over the Red Sea by Aaron was placed inside the ark of the covenant, which was carried by the Levites into the Jordan River to stop the waters. Just as the crossing of the Red Sea gave credibility to Moses and Aaron as leaders, so the crossing of the Jordan increased the people's confidence in Joshua, their new leader since Moses' death.

It seems this new generation of Israelites needed an experience of the same kind of deliverance their parents and ancestors had. Their experience was similar, but unique to their circumstances. Now this generation would have opportunities to tell their story to their children.

So, let us explore the effects of asking and telling. When a person asks a question there are at least two things that are implied: First, the person is curious and desires to know something new; and second, the person is willing to experience the change that might come from asking the question. There is a lot of power in the asking of questions, but also the potential to touch on something painful, though unknown. People who ask questions are important in the church, because sometimes the church assumes everyone knows something, and forgets to tell the story. Sometimes the church doesn't want to remember, but needs the reminder a question rouses. Questioners provide the push toward change and newness through their provocative questions.

I have made the necessity of questions plain, but what are the effects of hearing the story on those who ask? One is an increasing knowledge of one's history. Where do we come from? What happened that makes us bold in some areas? Why do we shy away from some topics? These questions all point to our collective history, a history that shapes us regardless of whether we are conscious of it or not. Asking questions shows a desire to become aware of the influences that have and will shape us. For a questioner, life doesn't just happen, it happens as we grow and struggle with its significance or seeming lack of significance.

There is a dangerous side to asking questions, because the stories we hear will call for a response. Are those who ask questions willing to change when they hear the answers? If I feel strongly about something at church, and ask a question of someone who has a different opinion than mine, am I willing to modify my opinion when I hear their answer, and the story behind their answer? Or, like our passage today, are we willing to live with different versions of the same story?

And what about those who tell the stories? What happens to them? When my grandma told me her stories, she relived the experiences by laughing, being solemn and even crying a few times. A story cannot be told dispassionately in order for it to result in experiential knowing. No—it must be told passionately, energized by the power of the story in our lives. To simply recite facts and dates is not much of a story, though they are part of the story. The power of a story comes through remembered detail and the impact it had on the teller.

Our story today seems to be a happy one, but we must remember that the Exodus and wandering in the wilderness included times of fear, uncertainty, mistrust, betrayal, and mourning. These feelings and experiences are recorded for us as part of the story, alongside the jubilation of being delivered from maltreatment and death into a covenant with Yahweh and a new land to call home.

So, there are risks in being a story-teller. Questions, however carefully phrased, can bring up difficult times and emotions. There is a cycle of pain's effects on us. We experience something difficult and we go through a hard time of coming to peace about it. After a struggle it seems we feel resolved about that issue. A year later we may encounter a reminder about that experience that brings the pain back to us in a new way, and we have to spend our time and energy sorting through it again.

It is important to realize we cannot face the full implications of traumatic events in our lives all at once. Instead we need to come back to the story over and over, leaving with something new after each telling. Each time we tell a story it will be from a different angle with different emphases, with different interpretations of "the facts." Just like in Joshua 4 where it seems there are two or three accounts of the same event, in any local church there are bound to be a hundred or so versions of any given story in our collective history. It is important to realize that questions enable us to come to terms with our history, both personal and corporate.

Something unnamed so far is the context for asking and telling. There is a relationship that holds the questions and stories. In our text the relationship is familial—children and descendants are to ask parents and ancestors. In the church we ask questions of God, and our brothers and sisters. It is being in relationship to someone that permits the vulnerability of exposing areas of ignorance, asking sensitive questions and being willing to experience the change that genuine questions foster. It is being in relationship that permits the vulnerability of exposing our unfinished agendas and the telling of our intimate stories of God's deliverance and care.

Revelation affects the future.

The occasion for the writing of the book of Joshua was the covenant between God and Israel and the **need**, flowing from that covenant, to keep alive the memories of the past in order both to perceive the significance of the present, and to open up vistas of the future (Woudstra. 1981, p. 17).

Both questions and stories create change, and hopefully encouragement, hope and healing, in the individuals who do the asking and telling, but also in the community which is the larger picture. Whatever changes we make in the present will influence the future. When we are drawn to God, the source, through a question or a story, we achieve new levels of understanding. Sometimes we are emotionally and spiritually healed. These eventual positive outcomes cause us to think more creatively and optimistically about the future, and energize us for the tasks at hand—to build visions and dream dreams for the future.

There are two effects of questions and stories on the future that I will name, but do not have time to develop. The first is that we build the future on tradition: we build new memorials beside the old ones and experience the cumulative effect of retelling stories that gain new and added meaning with time. Secondly, we build new traditions. When we hear one another's questions and stories, sometimes the best response is to develop something totally new.

Joshua 4 shows us that stories from the past have an effect on the present and the future. The stories of God's revelation to us in the Bible, through human story, provide us with insight and help us build relationships with God and others. Both questions and stories transform people, and provide hope and reassurance for the future.

Come, sisters and brothers, let us walk hand in hand, united by our experience of God in Christ, pushed to growth and greater faithfulness by one another's questions and stories.

ELAINE PINTO

Flexible Contentment

Philippians 4:10-23 NRSV

In the early part of this Century
    Louise Reimer, my maternal grandmother
       and her husband Jacob
    owned what was called a "Lauftje"
       (a dry goods store) in Russia.

Grandma Louise was a fairly well to do woman,
       full of romantic love for her husband
and known in the community for her generous spirit.
Characteristic of her
       were the songs of faith in God
            often on her lips.

But when the marauding bands heard she and her husband
    had given refuge
       to members of the fleeing Czar's family,
they tortured Jacob until he died.

They also had raided the store three times.
    And now my grandmother was left with four children
        - no possessions
and the worst economic disaster
        -no husband.

So while the children were carrying flowers
    to their father's grave

The church - wanting to help -
        pressed her into a marriage.
A widower with six children needed a wife.

Grandma fled with him to Canada
        but faced painful abuse in the marriage
        and yet more economic disaster.

Here in Winnipeg's North End,
        her adult children removed her from
                the abusive marriage.
        -As a result
she was removed from church membership,
        from communion, and fellowship.

        Left in economic, and now social poverty,
          -without a church
        she would sometimes come and slip in
            the back pews.
        But she didn't lose her song,
            even in these circumstances!

My mother recalls her grateful spirit:
        -the way she would lean out her rooming house window,
          with a full bowl of tomatoes from her tiny garden
          and call out to the neighbor
            "Look at this color!
Look at the gift God has given me!"

Grandmother Louise was a woman who had lived
        at both extremes of the economic and social scale.

In it all, in good and bad circumstances,
        she had peace and trust
          and retained a heart of steady worship.

        She had, what I would call a **flexible contentment**.

In Philippians 4:10-23,

Paul speaks of this kind of contentment
    He knew how to be content with little
        and with plenty.
    For him, there was a secret to that kind of living.

    As we listen in on this, Paul's most intimate letter,
        we're tempted to think that
            his Philippian friends
                were the reason for his contentment.

In verse 10, they were concerned for him;
    so concerned they searched for ways to meet his needs
        but couldn't reach him.

    Perhaps there were no persons going to Rome
        where he was imprisoned -
    Perhaps it was that Paul himself had
        stressed so often that he gathered money
        for other churches,
        not his own needs.
        (He made tents for that purpose
        and had given them a strong message that way.)

At any rate - they hadn't been able to make the connection
    to give him a personal gift before now.

Verse 15 tells us more about this loving church.
    They were the only ones to share in the financial
        cares of the churches that Paul ministered to.

    No church participated in the sufferings
    and the necessities, like these Philippians did.
    They were people who got into the habit of giving.

    I think we have people like that in this church.

But in regards to his contentment -

I. Paul says his well being was not determined by their gift.

This was not a plea for money
>Twice, in verses 11 and 17, he underlines it
>>..."Not that I am referring to being in need...
>>...Not that I seek the gift."

>Paul's need did not drive him to take or grasp
>>from people in a manipulative way.
>He didn't misuse the relationship
>as a soft touch for his own needs.

>In fact, he offers a strange reversal of facts
>>regarding gift-giving.

>He says in verses 17-19 that he's not the true recipient!
>>The gains are reversed!

>*Not that I seek the gift, but I seek the profit*
>>*that accumulates to your account.*
>*I have been paid in full and have more than enough;*
>>*I am fully satisfied, now that I have received from Epaphroditus*
>>>*the gifts you sent,*
>>>*a fragrant offering,*
>>>*a sacrifice acceptable and pleasing*
>>>*to God   (Phil. 4: 17, 18)*

Paul says three things about this
>reversal of facts regarding gift-giving.

Firstly, it's not to his profit - but to theirs.
>He says **they'll** really be the receivers - not him.

>He switches into accounting language here.
>>"Seek the profit" is a commercial phrase
>>>in the original.
>>In another translation - it reads:
>>"I desire fruit" that "may abound to your account."

Paul is speaking about results from something that is produced ...
- it can be measured.

Paul **did** gain by the gift,
but the permanent gain would be theirs.

Secondly, Paul tells them that though their gift was given to him
it was really received by the Lord.

He uses the worship language
of the Old Testament to describe this.

God **receives it** as a fragrant offering
a pleasing sacrifice to God.

These same words are used of Noah's offering (Gen. 8:21)
and of Levitical offerings of incense
in the tabernacle.
We also see this language in Revelation 8:3
where the incense of the prayers of the saints
are gifts that come up before the Lord.

Thirdly, there is the promise of God's supply.

And my God shall fully satisfy every **need** *of
yours according to his riches in glory
in Christ Jesus (Phil. 4:19).*

In our lives, maybe we really don't know what this means
because we keep getting tangled up
with what we think our needs are.

When Paul speaks about the Philippians' gifts,
as wonderful as these gifts were
and as wonderful as the gift-reversing rewards would be,
he says
"It's not that which gives me the power
to be content.

In sum - the secret of my contentment
is **not your provision for me.**

**II. The second thing Paul says is the secret of contentment
is not in the circumstances of his life**

We know that certainly couldn't be the case now for Paul.
He was writing from the loneliest place
in the world - a prison.
Maybe he was tempted to ask that same raw question
recorded in Matthew
that John the Baptist asked
from his prison cell-

"Are you the one, Lord Jesus ... are you the One?
Have I spent my life's energies
following One who is not really the Messiah?"

Paul did not have the comfort of a natural family to visit him.
And with no income from a livelihood
plus the costly appeals to Caesar,
he was likely very impoverished at this time.

His life was about to be put on the line
in a trial that could result in his death.
Yet he said he was content.

In poor circumstances
the temptation is to think of God as
One who won't come through for us.

But Paul didn't talk like this.

What Paul is saying is not that people don't get
provoked or anguished
over difficult circumstances,
but that there is a place of steadiness -
there is something that cannot be shaken.
There is an immovable factor

in our ever-changing lives.
It's strange, though, that when Paul says
circumstances don't determine his contentment,
he would mention another kind of circumstance:
-that of having plenty
being well-fed - everything going well.

Can the good life threaten real contentment too?

In Deuteronomy 8: 2-16 we read of a possible danger with living well.
One could forget God.

Just the way, when we are in dire circumstances
we're tempted to doubt God will do well by us-

So, when we are in good circumstances
we are tempted to assume God's goodness
is owed to us.

We are tempted to turn away from our true
source of contentment.

In this day of plastic money
is it sometimes
too easy to buy our way out of trouble?

In the day of plenty with countless
movies, videos, magazines, entertainment,
is it too easy to keep flooding our minds
and souls non stop -
with what does not bring contentment?

In this abundance of distractions
is it too easy to not take the time
to stop and listen
to the **real** need of our hearts?

-to invite and receive - again and again
the presence of the only One who satisfies?

For Paul, poor circumstances
        or abundance of things
        did not determine his equilibrium.
Neither affected how he lived in God.

Paul also gets at another facet
        of the circumstance problem
        by the way he repeats the contrasts three times in verse 12:
                little...plenty
                being well-fed...going hungry
                having plenty...being in need.

        It seems it's not just learning to endure being poor,
                or not just living faithfully in abundance -

It's also learning how to live with the
        unpredictability of circumstances
                -with situational change
        -with the **move** from one circumstance to the other.

Living well in God also
        means learning to live with tensions-
                with varying circumstances.

        This helps us to understand others in their circumstances.

The story is told of a fervent young monk
        who was learning to pray from the Psalms.

        He came to his wise old abbot to ask about a problem
                in his prayers.
        He found it difficult to say the positive Psalms
                on days when he was feeling low
                and wondered if he could not divide the Psalter.

        Could he say the 75 generally upbeat Psalms
                twice on his good days,
        and the other 75 Psalms twice on his bad days?
                This would fulfill his required 150 Psalms a day.

The wise old abbot told him
    that was exactly what he should **not** do.

"The praying of the Psalms is meant to remind us
    of joyful events when we are sad," he said,
        "and of tragedies when we are exuberant -

so that we may be taken out of
    our private little world
        and may become aware of others
            and their joys and hardships." (Demitrius Dumm. *Flowers in the Desert.*
                Paulist Press. 1987, p. 49)

To become caring people
    and to learn to move into contentment
        we need to **embrace transitions** from one
        circumstance to another...

because we are always moving,
        as one writer says
        "between days in which the whole world seems
            like a rose garden and days in which
                our hearts seem tied to a millstone." (Henri Nouwen. *Reaching Out.*
                Doubleday. 1975, p. 56)

Moving from one situation to another
        requires grace,
            that leads to contentment.

But even in this situation, Paul promises
        - despite change
        - despite having things or people one day
            and feeling destitute the next
        there still is the promise of contentment
because contentment does not rest in circumstances.

Paul still has one more step to go.

III. Thirdly, he says,

Contentment is not something you are born with,
it's something you have to learn.

Verses 11 and 12 repeat the phrase,
        "I have learned to be content...
        "I have learned the secret."
Paul did not come by this grace
        with his natural sunny disposition
          -it wasn't automatic.

        He had passed through great reverses in his life
          and grace is most needed with sudden reverses.

It was a grace he got
        plenty of opportunity to practice.

        While it's hard for us to learn to live equally
peacefully in good and bad circumstances;
        None of us want to **learn** that movement...
        the movement **between** bad and good circumstances-
          where the uncertainty in life needs to be embraced.

        We are people who want things resolved.
        As Henri Nouwen says
          some of us would prefer
           living with **a bad certainty**
             than with a good **un**certainty. (*Ibid.* p.74)

But Paul tells us that to **learn** this and to practice it
        is part of the process
          of becoming contented.

If the secret to Paul's contentment was not in his friends' gifts;
        If it was not in his circumstances;
        If it was not given to him by birth, and he had to learn it;
        What then, finally, was his secret?

IV. In verse 13 Paul says, "I can do all things,
through Christ who strengthens me."

There were some things for which Paul needed supernatural strength.

It was a mystery, a secret-
a living Person within would move with him
from one circumstance to the next.

Paul found that
though life is a journey of inconsistencies
and extremes in circumstance,
through Christ,
there was strength and power
to respond with peaceful steadiness.

If we were first or second century readers of this
letter we could easily see that verses 11 and 12 were
ordinary Stoic philosophy-
one of the ruling philosophies in Paul's day.

Stoicism said
Keep a stiff upper lip.
Learn to say, "I don't care".
Don't invest emotion when life gets difficult.

In fact, this word "content" was current in Stoicism
and was used to demonstrate the perfectly
self-sufficient person.

But Paul was a Christian.
He knew where he parted with the ways of Stoicism.
Paul was not self-sufficient,
he was **God-sufficient**.

"I can do all things **through Christ**
who strengthens me."
The empowerment of the Lord is what made
all the difference.

Paul was not simply the Stoic with the stiff upper lip.

He had a Keeper of his spirit,
the steady flame of the One within.
The Holy One
The Lord Jesus Christ
who would enable him.

How do we appropriate this kind of empowerment to find and keep contentment?

It's helpful to think of it like a marriage covenant.
It's both a one-time commitment
to receive God's loving presence
and a daily, hourly fresh renewal of it.
Perhaps we can visualize the empowering of
the Lord Jesus for the circumstances we're in now.

That steady grace is offered to you and me now.
We might hear it in the words of a song,
a Scripture,
a neighbor,
in creation.

Listen to the words the Lord speaks to us:
I love you today in this situation
I am with you and will keep you
in all places wherever you go.(Gen. 28:15)

I spoke of my Grandmother Louise in the beginning.

In her later years,
God gave her friends from a sister church
who embraced her in full communion.
She was restored in community life
and again she managed well economically.

But there was a steadiness that had threaded through all the
good and bad circumstances in her life-
a **flexible contentment**.

Her Lord and her song stayed the same.
One of the hymns that was never far
from her lips was
"So nimm denn meine Haende und fuehre mich."
("Take Thou my hand, oh Father, and lead Thou me.")

She exhibited what Paul says in the close of his letter
"The grace of the Lord Jesus Christ
be with your spirit."

For you and me too, there is a place of contentment
at the center of the heart of God
-not in our friend's provisions for us
-not in our good or bad circumstances.
And we're Not born with it -
it must be learned and appropriated.

It's in Christ.
In all the extremes of life
Let us rest in the steady flame
of the love of the Lord Jesus Christ.
Amen.

*All are witnesses
of God's redeeming love*

SARAH KLASSEN

Hagar and the God Who Sees

Genesis 16, 21:1-19

You may have noticed that this story is not a comfortable one. The plot involves a triangle in a household where there's not perfect harmony and, apparently, not enough love to go around; a household where jealousy and willfulness lead to cruel abuse. The setting shifts from the tents of this uneasy household to a hostile desert. The characters are not always nice people. And as for God's part in this story, I suspect if we had our way we'd want to discreetly rewrite the lines in certain places, modify God's role and bring it in line with our idea of what God should do. It's not an idyllic story for a mother's day, nor does it have an easy meaning, but it is a significant story.

Whose story is it that we've just heard? Usually we consider this to be a segment of Abram's story. Abram is the one God chose to covenant with, the one agonizing for an heir, the one we've come to see as everyone's favorite hero of faith. This morning we're going to acknowledge that people who are slaves, people who are foreigners, and people who are women have stories too, stories worth attending to. This time it's Hagar's story.

Perhaps, like me, you first heard this story in Sunday School. My teacher had us memorize the line, *"Thou God seest me."* (KJV) A more contemporary wording of this key to the story is "You are the God who sees me." Either way, that statement is pretty amazing: God the Creator sees you and me, personally, where we live, where we work, here where we sit in the pew. Is it comforting to think that God sees you? As a child I sometimes found the idea frightening and even now—it is sobering.

Who is Hagar? She's an Egyptian who has somehow come to live with a Hebrew family in the Promised land. Since the Egyptians were enemies of the Hebrews, she's definitely an outsider. She's a servant, a slave, with no rights and no freedom. She's a woman in a time and world where women did not enjoy an enviable status. She's also young and fertile.

Our story places Hagar side by side with a woman who is a Hebrew, one of God's people. Hagar's mistress, Sarah, is the wife of a prominent man and she is wealthy. As the story reveals, these advantages give her considerable power. She's also rather mean.

In this story, Hagar is given an important role, not uncommon in that culture. Like other female slaves before her, she's selected to become the solution to her mistress' infertility. This custom of using the female servant to ensure an heir, has been used by Margaret Atwood in her futuristic novel *The Handmaid's Tale (1986)*, in which a certain class of women, the handmaids, are kept in bondage in order to provide the sterile women of the privileged class with children. Atwood's story is a chilling one. And so is Hagar's. Phyllis Trible includes it as one of what she calls "texts of terror." *(Texts of Terror.* 1984)

The story is told in two main acts, and each act has two scenes, the first in the household of Abram and Sarah and the second in the desert.

In Genesis 16, Sarah takes the initiative and gives Hagar to Abram. It seems to have been Sarah's idea and her motive, if we read her words carefully, seems to be more immediate, more self-centered than that God's will should be done or that the promise of becoming a large nation can be fulfilled. "Perhaps I can build a family through her," she says. Sarah wants a family; **she** wants desperately to be saved from the terrible affliction of childlessness. And Abram has no objections.

The plan works. But instead of being delighted that a child is to be born, Sarah is upset. Hagar, the subservient one, is quite willing to grab her chance to feel superior. **She's** the pregnant one; not her mistress. The story says that "she began to despise her mistress." Another translation uses the word "contempt." Despise and contempt are not nice words. Sarah did not like to be despised; it made her furious. She blamed the whole thing, which had been her idea in the first place, on Abram. "You are responsible for the wrong I am suffering." And did Abram dig in his heels and insist on fair and just treatment for the pregnant maid? No. He said, "Do with her whatever you think best."

And then we read these disappointing words: *"Then Sarah mistreated Hagar; so she fled."*

This is clearly a case of abuse and it happens in a family situation to one who is powerless. We can't, of course, come down too hard on Abram and Sarah for keeping slaves and using the handmaiden as a concubine: in that cultural context both practices were legal and acceptable. But the heartless way they treat her appalls us: the failure to treat as human a person who, though she's different from the rest of the family, has feelings and sensibilities, has the capacity for being hurt, and is in a very vulnerable situation. One can imagine the desolation, pain, anger, and perhaps fear, evoked by this mistreatment. If we could enter into Hagar's suffering and loneliness and try to feel the callousness that surrounds her, we might be moved to resolve with God's help never again to reject a person who isn't in the inner circle, who hasn't had the advantages we've had, not even if that person hasn't shown us perfect respect. Then the world in which we live and move would be a different place, and reading the story would have been worthwhile.

But back to the story and the language of the story. When we relate to people, we do so through language, through words. Ursula le Guin, science fiction writer, suggests that as we grow up we learn first a mother tongue and later a father tongue. The mother tongue, she suggests, the one we learn first, is the common language of everyday things. It is language that expects an answer; it is language not just to communicate information but also for relationship, to make friends, to encourage someone. It is language that unites and brings us closer together. The father tongue which we learn later is the language of command and control, the language of pronouncement, the language of social power. It is language that distances. It has the power to displace the mother tongue.

It seems to me that both Abram and Sarah are speaking with the second kind of language: "Go, sleep with my maid servant," "You are responsible," "The Lord judge between you and me." "Do with her whatever you think best." This isn't the kind of language that invites Hagar into conversation. She remains voiceless in this scene.

Ursula le Guin, in commenting on power, differentiates between power **over** and power **to**. The first gives you control and the second leaves you with responsibility. In this story the mistress has power **over** her maid and she exercises it with unnecessary cruelty.

Hagar, who has no controlling kind of power, still has power **to** and so she chooses to run away. Like us, she has to take responsibility for her choices. Where does Hagar's choice lead? It leads her to the desert.

And this brings us to the second scene of the first act where God enters the story, through the messenger, and where Hagar gets into the conversation. In the desert where God sees Hagar, God begins by using the mother tongue kind of language. For starters, God addresses her by name, something her master and mistress never do in this story. They talk about her, as if she's an object. But God calls her by name.

God, speaking through his messenger, asks a question which invites an answer. *"Hagar, servant of Sarah, where have you come from, and where are you going?"* If **we** were writing the story we might leave out that bit about "servant of Sarah." Did the angel have to rub it in? Hadn't she run away from her mistress? Wasn't she free now of that bondage?

Hagar, drawn into conversation with the divine, answers the first part of the question: "Where have you come from?" She says, very honestly, "I'm running away from my mistress."

Here we would like the angel to say something like: "Good for you. You've escaped an impossible situation and it's about time. Don't worry about a thing. I'll help you." Instead, the divine messenger answers the second part of the question, the part Hagar left unanswered, maybe because she wasn't sure of the answer: "Where are you going?" The messenger tells her where she's going. *"Go back to your mistress and submit to her."* This is not mother tongue and surely the command flies in the face of reason, to send the abused victim back into a situation of abuse. Can that be God's will? What is this story about, anyway? Is its moral simply: Don't run away from your problems, face up to them? Is the divine message designed to save Hagar's life, and her unborn child's, because they would surely perish in the desert? Or does the story have to do somehow with the fact that God's plan is greater and more complex than we will ever understand? That's an easy explanation which is often used when we're baffled.

We wish the story would go on to say that when Sarah saw her handmaiden return, she relented and treated her kindly at least for the remainder of the pregnancy. We are given no such comfort.

Let's return to the rest of this scene in the desert. God does have something remarkable to say to Hagar. He tells her: *"I will so increase your descendants that they will be too numerous to count."* Doesn't that sound like the way God spoke to Abram? This sounds like covenant language: God entering into covenant with his creation. But with a woman? An Egyptian—one of the enemies of God's people? A slave? The divine messenger tells Hagar her future. God knows her future, as he knows the future of the patriarchs and the future of his chosen, special people, the

Hebrews. Hagar may not be inside that special covenant between God and his special people, but she **is** part of God's creation and God's ultimate purpose embraces everything that has been created. Hagar is in God's plan.

God lets Hagar know the good with the bad. Yes, she will have a son and be the mother of many descendants, that's the good news. But her son will live in hostility and is promised no land. That's the significant bad news.

Hagar in the desert: an image pregnant with possibility. She foreshadows the history of the Hebrews in reverse. **They** found themselves in the desert when they were fleeing **from** Egypt, and they were desperate for water. **She** is apparently fleeing **into** Egypt, which is home to her, and the story tells us she's near a spring. She **has** water. We are reminded that Jesus too found himself in the desert for a period of very hard testing. And we sometimes refer to bad times as desert experiences.

Hagar met God in the desert. God didn't take her to a beautiful oasis and assure her she didn't have to return to an unkind mistress and to a master who wouldn't take her side. But he **saw** her there, he **knew** who she was, he spoke her name and made her a promise no other woman in the Bible is given. God acknowledged this Egyptian slave woman whom his people had mistreated. And apparently God didn't act because she pleaded so desperately, the way we sometimes pray. As far as the story goes, Hagar did **not** call out for God. God spoke first. He didn't have to, but he did what it is his nature to do: look for the lost. And she finds her voice in the desert and acknowledges "You are the God who sees me." In saying this, she becomes an individual in the Bible who names God. We would like the story to tell us that from this moment Hagar

put her complete trust in God and followed him faithfully for the rest of her life. We aren't told whether or not that happened. But Hagar's last words in this segment of the story are strong words. She says: *"I have now seen the One who sees me."* Hagar's eyes had been opened. Things have changed.

And now the sequel, which we pick up after much has happened. Hagar gives birth to a son: Ishmael. Then Sarah gives birth to a son: Isaac. Abram can breathe easy; he's got the heir he so desperately wanted. And Sarah can hold her head high. They've probably regretted their earlier impatience that resulted in that whole messy business with Hagar, but God has given them a legitimate son and all is well

And once again Sarah uses her power, not to show kindness, but to control. The Egyptian slave has got to go. The son of the servant may not grow up with Sarah's son, and he may certainly not inherit along with that son. Abram, to give him credit, is distressed with his wife's decision, not enough to take drastic action, but enough to pack some bread and water for the outcasts.

Maybe the most frightening thing in the story is that God tells Abram to listen to his wife. Why? Is it because the covenant is above all else? God chose Abram and Sarah to be parents of a special people. Hagar wasn't chosen for this privilege. Is it because God with his complete view sees more than one way for Hagar? Can God be on more than one side in a conflict? Or is Hagar the victim doomed to live out indefinitely the hurtful results of the unwise decisions taken by her all-too-human master and mistress, who occupy positions of privilege?

In any case, Hagar finds herself once more in the desert, this time not by her own choice, this time with a young child, and this time the story offers no spring of water. The small supply of water she carries will not last long. The situation is desperate.

Our Egyptian Hagar places her child under a bush because she can't bear to see him die. God who lacks neither the ability to see nor the ability to hear, once again acts even before Hagar prays. God responds to the cries of Hagar's child, and opens Hagar's eyes so she can see the spring of water nearby. This is a saving God who does not let the abused woman and the rejected child die in the desert. Hagar is assured once again that she has a future, a future known to God. She is offered hope. She is not left sobbing on the ground. As the story concludes she is picking herself up and getting water for her thirsty child.

The novelist John Steinbeck once said: "If a story is not about the hearer he [she] will not listen......A great and lasting story is about everyone or it will not last. The strange and foreign is not interesting - only the deeply personal and familiar." (*East of Eden*. Viking Penquin. 1970, p.310)

Is Hagar's story about us? It has certainly lasted. We may be unwilling to identify with the "villains" of the story—the Hebrew master and mistress; and some of us may feel we have nothing in common with the foreign slave woman.

Our faith community is one that God is blessing locally, and also within the global context; we are in a position of privilege, and that gives us power. How do we use that power in the church and in the larger community? Do we use it to bring hope and good news and practical help to the world? Or do we withhold friendship and increase suffering?

This story is about family. We have lots to learn about family, whether that's the biological family or the church family or the community. We need to learn about extending family boundaries to make room for those who are not one of us, for those we deem too ungifted to have anything to offer, for those we have no place for because somehow they don't attract us, or they are "different," and we see them as alien. Possibly no one else wants them either. And yet they are looking to be called out of their desert of loneliness, fear, abuse and rejection, into a warm family.

Maybe some of us identify this morning with Hagar. Which one of us hasn't at some time, perhaps this very week, felt like an outsider, a stranger, rejected and unloved, or found ourselves stranded in a desert, perhaps of our own making, or a desert we've been dropped into by circumstances, or one that we've been driven into by a callous world. What an amazing thing to know that in that desert, God, who is a God who sees and saves, knows about us, and if we are desperate enough, and willing to listen, we may hear God speak to us in a way that has never happened in better days. He can open our eyes and teach us, too, to see him. And that's a miracle.

The man in the gospel of John, after meeting God in human form, testified: *"One thing I do know. I was blind but now I see."* As we pick ourselves up from our deserts and move toward the springs of water that God is showing us, we too can say with Hagar, *"I have now seen the One who sees me."* That possibility is good news.

NADINE FRIESEN

Hannah's Journey from Hopelessness to Hopefulness

I Samuel 1-2

Hannah's drama includes feelings, experiences and thoughts that most of us have had at one time or another:
• Enduring ridicule for something over which we have no control. Maybe it's something about our appearance - some family characteristic - having to take a job that has little respect - some activity we can't do well, no matter how hard we try.
• Questioning why other people's prayers are answered when God seems too busy or indifferent to respond to our needs. Wondering why God doesn't change things if God really has the power to do so.
• Wanting desperately to do or give something to someone we love dearly - but it seems so impossible, we feel so inadequate.
• Being so discouraged about life's disappointments we don't even want to eat.
• Constantly bumping into people all around us who have exactly what we so desperately want and wondering what would be wrong with us having it also.

Our common experiences certainly are not all negative.
• Being amazed and delighted at God's goodness and faithfulness in the midst of all the challenges and struggles life can offer.
• Knowing we are loved for who we are, not for what we can or can't do.
• Feeling the thrill of having a prayer of many years answered unexpectedly.
• If you have not experienced these things personally, you probably know someone who has. All of them were a part of Hannah's story which is found in I Samuel 1-2.

Setting

The time is about 1075 BC and Israel is in transition between judges and kings. The place is Ramathaim or Ramah, a few miles north of Jerusalem. The characters include Elkanah, the husband, and Hannah and Peninnah, his two wives. The plot is based on the fact that Peninnah has children - Hannah doesn't. Hannah is Elkanah's favorite and Peninnah was probably added because Hannah didn't have children.

Act I - Journey Without Hope

Elkanah and his family were faithful worshipers. Every year they went to Shiloh, Israel's center of worship. This was where Eli and his sons served as priests. When it was time to sacrifice, Elkanah would dole out the sacrifices.

Peninnah's portion was large because she received some for all her sons and daughters. Hannah was only Hannah so her portion was smaller but note in verse 5, *"because of Elkannah's love for her, he gave her a double portion."*

Not that she needed any reminders, but the portions were a constant reminder to Hannah that she had no children. That pain was intensified by Peninnah's taunts. "You don't have any children." "You haven't given Elkanah a son." "I have both sons and daughters."

Every year - over and over. It certainly would dampen one's joy in worship; one wonders why Hannah even went. How would you feel if as you entered the sanctuary people would remind you of all that's lacking in your life?

> *Whenever Hannah went up to the house of the Lord, her rival provoked her till she wept and would not eat. (I Samuel 1:7)*

Elkanah's response was loving and supportive. "Hannah why are you crying? Don't you know I love you? Don't worry about giving me sons. Don't I mean more to you than ten sons?"

On one of these trips to Shiloh, Hannah pours out her heart to God and makes a dramatic promise. It sounds like one of those "Lord if you'll just get me out of this mess, I'll go be a missionary in the jungle" kind of prayers.

> *In bitterness of soul Hannah wept much and prayed to the Lord. And she made a vow, saying, "O Lord Almighty, if you will only look upon your servant's misery and remember me, and not forget your servant but give her a son, then I will give him to the Lord for all the days of his life, and no razor will ever be used on his head." (vv. 1:10,11)*

She already had enough trouble - feeling inadequate, knowing that not having children was viewed as divine judgment, having to watch all the people coming as families to a great celebration, and dealing with the harassment of her "co-wife." Now on top of all that, when she goes to pray, the pastor thinks she is drunk.

This may seem like Eli's most embarrassing ministry moment. In reality it was not all that uncommon to find intoxicated people in the temple where there was frequent celebrating and feasting. This was also a time of spiritual lethargy for Israel when the focus was more on personal pleasure than on worship and obedience to God. Sound a bit familiar? Eli's response was to wish her God's peace and the answer to her prayer.

Note Hannah's next step.

> *She said, "May your servant find favor in your eyes." Then she went her way and ate something, and her face was no longer downcast. Early the next morning they arose and worshiped before the Lord and then went back to their home at Ramah. (vv. 18-19)*

Hannah's Response

Before going on to Act II, let's review Hannah's response at this point.
• She was **honest about her feelings** and expressed her hurt.
• She **didn't fight back.**
• She **took her pain to the Lord.** Her despair was directed to the One with ultimate power and compassion.

> *And without faith it is impossible to please God, because anyone who comes to him must believe that he exists and that he rewards those who earnestly seek him. (Heb. 11:6)*

She went to the Lord, not knowing what her reward would be.
- She **viewed herself as a servant**, in submission to the Lord Almighty.
- She **made a promise**, a vow. Maybe she was hoping it would aid in the fulfillment of her request.

Nevertheless, she was willing to offer back to the Lord what He gave to her. That is an **act of obedience**.

It seems that this is the time when hopelessness began turning to hopefulness; not when the problem was solved but when she surrendered her despair to the Lord Almighty.

Our Response

How do we respond when we are full of anguish and deeply troubled? It seldom works to try to cover up the pain. It reveals itself in one way or another. We need to share our struggles with one another to help lighten the load. We also need to recognize that ultimately there is only One true burden bearer. Christ invites us to bring our burdens to the cross and leave them there.

May the God of hope fill you with all joy and peace as you trust in him, so that you may overflow with hope by the power of the Holy Spirit. (Romans 15:13)

The joy, peace and hope come - not as all problems are solved - but as we trust in Him.

Act II - Journey Toward Hope

Elkanah lay with Hannah his wife, and the Lord remembered her. So in the course of time Hannah conceived and gave birth to a son.

She named him Samuel, saying "Because I asked the Lord for him." (vv. 19b-20)

Hannah stayed home during the trips to Shiloh for the next few years, probably until Samuel was three years old. From other literature written at this time we know children were usually weaned at that age. Imagine the mixed emotions and dynamics Hannah must have felt in making this journey. The joy of answered prayer combined with the agony of anticipated separation.

The Nazarite vow she had made meant that Samuel was specially dedicated to God and would separate himself from others and submit to God. It included outward signs such as abstaining from wine, cutting of hair and contact with dead bodies.

Hopefully, there was no ridicule during this trip. Hannah and Elkanah brought a significant sacrifice as indicated in verse 24, a full grown bull and a half bushel of flour and wine. After making the sacrifice, they presented their son to Eli, giving God the credit for Samuel's existence.

Hannah's Response

Some think Hannah was just a person more concerned with her own reputation than with truly seeking the Lord. I'm not sure any of us ever have totally pure motives. The miracle is that God continues to work out His plan in spite of us. There are several key principles we can learn from Hannah's response.

1. Hannah's dedication of her son was an **act of gratitude** to God in praise for answered prayer.

2. She viewed Samuel as a **gift from God** on loan to them. Not a bad way for all parents to view their children. He had come from God in the first place and now he was going back to the

house of God to live and serve.

3. Hannah **trusted God**. He cared about her and would care for her son as well. There is no greater place of security than in the care of God. Hannah had learned to trust through her pain. Rather than becoming bitter, her relationship with God had deepened.

4. God gave her the **strength to obey** and enabled her to carry out his plan even though Hannah didn't understand all the implications. God was already preparing Samuel for the ministry he had for him. God knew about his plan for Israel as a nation and through them, all of the world. A world in which each person, including you and me, would have an opportunity to respond to Jesus Christ.

Hannah's story is evidence again that while God is concerned about the affairs of the nations and the entire world, he is just as involved in the lives of each individual.

Hannah's Prayer

The prayer attributed to Hannah in chapter 2:1-10 describes her expression of confidence in the power of God. God invites us to apply Hannah's prayer to whatever it is in our lives that we need or want to dedicate or rededicate to God.

> *My heart rejoices in the Lord; in the Lord my horn is lifted high. (v. 1)*

Relying on God takes a big weight off our shoulders and renews our strength.

> *My mouth boasts over my enemies, for I delight in your deliverance.*

Our enemy may be a critical spirit, a temper that takes off easily or a nagging worry we can't let go.

Verses 2 through 5 describe the character of God. No one compares to God who is our Rock and stability. God is all knowing and has the final word, even though we sometimes act like we know it all. All that we are that is good is a gift from God.

God's actions are described in verses 6 through 10. God gives strength to the weak. He lifts the lowly and offers protection.

> *It is not by strength that one prevails; those who oppose the Lord will be shattered. He will thunder against them from heaven; the Lord will judge the ends of the earth. (vv. 9b, 10)*

Our Response

Like Hannah, we need God's help to make the journey from hopelessness to hopefulness. Like Hannah, we can decide whether or not to believe and act upon the truths that sometimes we feel and sometimes we don't.

There is great security in belonging to an all-powerful God. God knows what He is doing. He deserves the credit for all that is good. God's plan and glory can be revealed even through pain and hurt. Circumstances do not change the character of God. God can be trusted with whatever is committed to Him. Hope comes when we surrender control to God.

Where are you on your journey from hopelessness to hopefulness?

Wherever there is God, there is hope.

> *We who have fled to take hold of the hope offered to us may be greatly encouraged. We have this hope as an anchor for the soul, firm and secure. Let us hold unswervingly to the hope we profess, for he who promised is faithful. (Heb. 6:18,19; 10:23)*

A Fish, A Vine and A Worm: The Way to Jonah's Heart

Jonah

When I was asked to share from the book of Jonah, I imagined I would discover truths concerning running from God, mercy, or prejudice and racism, but God impressed on my mind and heart that Jonah is a story about God's personal and persistent concern for his people, his messengers. Jonah is the only book among the prophets in the Old Testament in which the focus is on the messenger, not on the message. The book of Jonah has taught me a lot about myself, and what it is that God really wants from me and what he wants to do in me.

Let me begin by telling you a little of my personal story. You'll see how it connects with Jonah later.

I spent the first 18 years of my life in Lethbridge, Alberta. Then after two years of Bible School in British Columbia, and one year in Holland with MCC, I returned home for one year before going to Tabor College in Hillsboro, Kansas. It was while I was studying at Tabor College that one of the professors challenged me to go to inner city Los Angeles on a three week course during the month of January. It was after that trip that I was invited to move to L.A. as a full-time missionary. I fought it for a while, but

God persuaded me through the needs, through what I knew I had to offer because of my family and church background, and through a deepening assurance that he would be with me.

Three months after I moved to L.A. in January of 1973, I was asked to become the women's staff director. That was a much tougher decision. By that time our home had been robbed, people thought we belonged to the house of prostitution behind our home (why else would white women be living there?), our windows had been broken repeatedly, a young guy had been killed on our cross street, a badly beaten woman came to my door for help after an attempted rape ... So, being asked to direct the ministry and staff was not like asking me to go for a walk in the park. I knew what kinds of things could happen.

I wrestled and agonized over the decision. I remember how one afternoon I spent hours walking back and forth in my bedroom, praying, talking out loud, arguing for and against accepting the responsibility—but mostly I remember a deep awareness that this was going to be a very lonely and difficult position at times. I was tempted to run like Jonah did. During that period of my life I received a letter from the former pastor of this church which included the verses from Joshua 1: 6 and 9, *"Be strong and courageous, because you will lead these people ... do not be terrified or discouraged, for the Lord your God will be with you wherever you go."* I realized this letter was a personal message from God since the writer didn't know about my struggle at the time.

As you probably guessed, I finally said "yes." That was 22 years ago. But, my sense was correct. Leadership was tough. Only a few months later we received numerous threatening calls because I had finally called the police when someone repeatedly broke into our garage. The parents were furious that their sons had police records because of that call.

One afternoon after repeated threats of dismemberment, I told God I was not leaving my bedroom until he gave me peace—I was exhausted by the fear. It was up to God to do something or I would have to leave L.A. God did in fact meet me—he showed me that no matter what they did to my body, they could never touch the real me. Also, it was as clear as crystal to me that I could not create peace—peace is a fruit of the Spirit. Also, peace is not the absence of danger. It's the presence of God. I opened my hands and mind and heart, and I received peace. Many times after that, particularly when I counseled women who had been attacked or raped, we found the supernatural gift of peace by asking for it, by receiving it—we could not create or manufacture it.

These stories from my life show you how God called me, communicated with me and kept working on my heart. I've had many similar experiences with God over the years. Each time a new challenge came, or I wanted to run, God stuck with me and kept working on me and in me.

By now you may have an idea of what I think God is saying through the book of Jonah. Let's look at a few things about God and a few things about Jonah that will lead us to the core or central issues of this text. Let's look at God first.

God communicated with Jonah personally

God called Jonah to a specific task and spoke to Jonah in such a way that Jonah knew it was God who was speaking. We read in chapter 1, verse 1, *"The word of the Lord came to Jonah son of Amittai: 'Go to the great city of Nineveh and preach against it.'"* Jonah knew God was speaking to him personally, and he knew what God wanted him to do.

God knew which lessons Jonah needed to learn. Jonah was a Jewish prophet during a time when the Ninevites and the larger race of Assyrians were not only living wicked lives, they were also enemies of the Jews. Jonah likely had memories of Jews who had been tortured and killed by the Assyrians. These memories made Jonah pretty angry. In addition there was a growing problem among the Jewish people. They forgot that God had chosen them specifically so they could bless other nations—he had not simply chosen them so they could be blessed. The Jews had become self-centered.

Jonah too had become exclusive—he wanted God's mercy and blessing for himself and his people, but not for their enemies; he was actually racist—he wanted judgment and justice instead of mercy for the enemies of God. Jonah had become bitter, angry, selfish, and self-protective. God knew he would have to teach Jonah step by step, but God was persistent and he communicated in ways that Jonah understood.

Throughout the story, God obviously knows Jonah's learning style. Jonah must have been a tactile or kinesthetic learner, someone who learned through his senses. God used all of Jonah's senses by using a great wind, a violent storm, a fish, a three-day trip inside the stomach of a sea creature, a sensational ride through the air (I can only imagine what it would feel like to be vomited out of a fish), a vine, nice cool shade, a scorching east wind and even a worm. Jonah had a chance to see, hear, touch, taste, and smell things he'd never dreamed of. Yes, God got Jonah's attention by communicating in ways Jonah would understand.

So now we know three things about God—he communicated personally, knew which lessons Jonah needed to learn, and taught Jonah in ways Jonah could understand. But what was God's purpose in all this? Was God simply trying to save Nineveh? Let's look now at Jonah to gain further insights as to what this story means for us.

Not only did God know Jonah, Jonah knew God too; well, at least he knew a lot about him

Sometimes we think that people who run away from God don't know him. On the contrary, Jonah knew God all too well. Jonah heard God's call and directions. Otherwise he wouldn't have run. In chapter 1 he tells the sailors that God is Lord of the sea and dry land. And in chapter 4 he accuses God of being *"gracious and compassionate, slow to anger and abounding in love, a God who relents from sending calamity"* (4:2). Yes, Jonah knew about God.

Jonah also knew that God was a God of mercy. Wasn't that why he was against going to Nineveh? He didn't want to warn the people. So, when the terrible storm came up on the sea, Jonah knew that this God of mercy could very well stop the storm. They wouldn't have had to throw Jonah into the sea. In other words, Jonah

could have repented right then and there, and the storm would have stopped. But Jonah was so set against God showing mercy to the wicked people of Nineveh he would rather die than be a messenger of God's mercy to his enemies. He was willing to sacrifice his life so the Ninevites would get what was coming to them, what they deserved. Anger is that consuming; bitterness has that kind of power. Jonah would rather die than let God be merciful.

Yes, Jonah knew a lot about God. But that wasn't enough. Jonah also knew God was among his people. For a moment Jonah may have thought that by getting out of the land of God's chosen people, he could silence the voice of God. Don't we make the same assumption at times? If we can skip hearing God at the youth group or in church, if we can hang out with the crowd who are having fun and who don't ever talk about God, maybe God will stop bugging us. That's possibly what Jonah thought.

So when God says, go north east, Jonah goes south west. The opposite direction. If your mother has ever said, "Go upstairs to do your homework and you slip downstairs to watch television, you're playing Jonah's game. Except it wasn't a game, was it? The opposite direction in Jonah's case was literally **down**. Not only does Jonah head **down** to Joppa, he goes **down** below the deck on the ship. He has no idea how far **down** he's going to go before this trip is over. Later when he's praying inside the fish he prays words *"from the depths of the grave," "you hurled me into the deep, into the very heart of the seas," "the deep surrounded me", "to the roots of the mountains I sank down"* (2: 2-6). When Jonah went the opposite direction, he went down. Maybe the opposite direction isn't all that safe. Who wants to go **down** in life?

No, you don't get away from God by running away from God's people. So far we've learned that Jonah knew about God and he knew that God was among his people. What else do we know about Jonah? Jonah even knew how to pray.

From inside the fish Jonah calls out to the Lord in his distress and God answers and listens to his cry (2:2). Verses 4 and 7 show Jonah also knew where to find God—in his holy temple— that's where God met Israel in those days. Throughout the prayer Jonah goes back and forth between expressions of pain at being so far down, and expressions of knowing where God is.

The prayer actually sounds a lot like me when I'm at my lowest point—I can almost hear myself crying out to God and interjecting a "but I know you're there" and then arguing and complaining some more and saying, "but you've promised, God," and after a few more gut-wrenching expressions I'll add, "aren't you supposed to be a loving heavenly father?" Perhaps you also know and pray this kind of prayer.

Unfortunately, in Jonah's case, (and often in mine) prayer was totally self-centered. Even inside the fish he never once mentions the Ninevites. He uses the words "I" "me" "my" and "mine" at least 18 times according to my count. Regardless of the self focus, we have to remember that Jonah did pray.

But, knowing about God and praying honestly are not enough. God wants something else from Jonah. Is it obedience God is after?

In chapter 3 Jonah obeys

After Jonah gets out of the fish, God does say a second time, "Go to Nineveh" and Jonah obeys. But look at the message Jonah brings Nineveh in chapter 3 verse 4! *"Forty more days and Nineveh will be destroyed."* No hopeful word about repentance, no testimony of how God spared his life in the fish when he disobeyed, not a whisper about the mercy of God—only judgment. You get the feeling Jonah is obeying but that he hasn't changed much. God's messengers often take a long time to change, especially when it comes to our feelings about other races and other groups who are not only different than we are, but particularly if their sins threaten our safety or jeopardize our children directly.

I've felt it myself in Los Angeles. When I'm scared because of the violence, the repeated thefts, the many rapes—my fear and anger boils up and I don't even want mercy for some of the wicked, or people who abuse women and children.

I've heard it on a larger scale as well. There was sort of a gleeful attitude about God finally giving Los Angeles what it deserved when we had the riots, the fires, and the earthquake—all within these past three years. Yes, instead of begging for mercy, Christians gloat about judgment, as long as it's others who are getting "what they deserve," not us. I'm not suggesting God's justice is never expressed through judgment. Nor am I forgetting that God's mercy on Nineveh came **after** they repented.

And Nineveh did repent. They were given a 40 day warning, but immediately they *"declared a fast, and all of them, from the greatest to the least, put on sackcloth and sat in the dust"* (3:5,6). Their immediate repentance is very different from Jonah's repeated delays. *"When God saw what they did and how they turned from their evil ways, he had compassion and did not bring upon them the destruction he had threatened"* (3:10).

Now that Jonah has obeyed, it appears God's work is done—Nineveh has repented, God's judgment has been delayed, and God's mercy has been experienced. So the book could end. But, here's the clincher of the story. God did not only want Jonah's obedience. In other words, **he did not simply want Jonah so he could use him.** What? Can it be that knowing about God, praying to him, and even obeying aren't really what God is after in Jonah? What does God want? God is after Jonah's heart. God wants Jonah's heart to be like God's heart—filled with mercy.

And at this point it still isn't. Jonah is still angry. Maybe he's angry because he hates the Ninevites so much he wants them dead. Maybe he's angry because he thinks God's chosen people deserve health, wealth, and prosperity while the wicked should get sickness, poverty, and suffering. Maybe he's angry because he could look like a false prophet whose words don't come true—his job may be on the line if it's proven that his predictions as a prophet don't come true. Perhaps it's all of these.

But watch how God persists in trying to get Jonah's heart to change. It's after Nineveh repents, after Jonah's job is done, that we see most dramatically what God desires. He takes a whole chapter, chapter four, to do this. God could have said, "Forget it, Jonah, you'll never change." Instead, since Jonah's not understanding the lesson, God decides to show him once more that the real problem is Jonah's heart. Watch how God does it.

It's real hot. God causes a vine to grow quickly in order to provide shade for Jonah. Jonah is ecstatic—his needs are being met. He is enjoying God's provision and mercy—for himself. But without warning, along comes one very greedy worm—and the shade is gone. On top of that a scorching wind whips up. Jonah is boiling hot—inside and out. He is mad enough to die.

And, one final time in the story, the loving compassionate God, the personal and persistent God, tries to teach Jonah the whole point with a story that Jonah can understand. He says, "Look, here you are Jonah, you care about a plant that dies, a plant that you didn't even create. Can't you see that I have the right to care about people and animals that I in fact did create?" In other words, "You want the plant to live because it gives you shade and comfort. I want 120,000 people and their cattle to live because I created them, because I love them. Shouldn't I take care of them?"

That's where the book ends. How embarrassing! Jonah cares more about a plant than about 120,000 people. Did Jonah catch on? Did Jonah repent? Did his heart change? We don't know for sure. I assume he did or he wouldn't have told his story to the press. How else would the author have learned about Jonah running away, about the fish, the prayer, the repentance of the people of Nineveh and even the vine? That would be embarrassing material to leak out if your heart hadn't changed.

Jesus Teaches the Same Lesson

In case we are tempted to think that only Jonah needed this change of heart, Jesus tells numerous stories and parables with the same message. The parable of the unmerciful servant in Matthew 18:23-35, portrays someone who has received enormous forgiveness from his master but is unwilling to forgive his fellow servant a petty debt. The unmerciful servant is like Jonah.

In the parable of the prodigal son in Luke 15:11-32, the elder brother begrudges the prodigal his undeserved forgiveness. Here the elder brother is like Jonah.

The story of the Pharisee and the tax collector in Luke 18:9-14, shows how the tax collector, like the Ninevites, hopes and prays against all odds, "God be merciful to me a sinner", while the Pharisee, like Jonah, remains proud and self-righteous.

And finally, the parable of the laborers in the vineyard in Matthew 20:1-16, hits us hard when it describes how those who served all day are angry when those who work only one hour receive the same pay. Inside we resent God's generous mercy toward those who have known less about God, have prayed less, and done less often than we have.

Yes, the lesson needs to be learned over and over—otherwise it wouldn't be repeated in both Testaments would it? Yes, God wants our hearts to be like his own—that's why he communicates personally with us, teaching us the lessons we need to learn, in ways we can understand.

Personal Illustration

So, in my preparation of this sermon, I decided to go back to me. I decided to tell you the truth about how God is trying to change my heart even now. I started this sermon by telling you how I wrestled with God—but how he kept working in my heart throughout my years in L.A. Well, I have to confess that I blew it at times too—but God has been personal and persistent with me just as he was with Jonah. About 4 years ago, after 18 years in Los Angeles, I was exhausted, discouraged, and even angry. I felt I had given everything I had to give. I had nothing left in me. Many things about the city, about my relationships, about the organization, and even about myself seemed hopeless. I had no idea at the time that God was using these feelings and experiences to show me how much he cared about my heart and about me personally.

I was offered a study leave and decided to go to Fuller Seminary. I can not begin to tell you in how many ways God spoke to my heart, but he had his storms and fish and vines and worms in my life too. Through professors, courses, friends, and fellow-missionaries, God communicated understanding, affirmation and correction. Through family and supporters, through the beauty of nature, and through times of solitude and reflection, God has kept on changing and restoring my heart. The beauty is that as God is changing me, he's giving people in the city more courage to let him work in their hearts too.

How is it that God changes our hearts? What happens if after we've known God, prayed, and obeyed God, we still have anger and bitterness? In my life God works on my heart through kindness and affirmation, through unexpected blessings and expressions of unconditional love, through affirming my gifts and my person. God also uses my failures and weaknesses—those times when I can do nothing but call for help, when I see my sinfulness, and my need for mercy. God changes my heart through the times when there is so much death and sadness around me that I can do nothing else but turn to God, unable to give anything but simply needing to receive. In silence I open my heart, my hands, and my mind for filling. I wait in God's presence, accepting comfort; I simply sit there listening, instead of telling or asking or planning my agenda. The kind of trust needed to allow God to change my heart is in many ways a gift from God. It's hard to resist God's personal and loving persistence!

And so, when God recently asked me to stay at the seminary longer, to continue writing, teaching, training and counseling, rather than moving back into full-time ministry in L.A., I started to argue but I also listened. First I said, "I'm not smart enough. It's too much money. It's too lonely to get a Ph.D. There are too many needs in the city to take time out for more studies." But, God sent his fish and vines and worms again.

He confirmed this call through people in the city who want me to represent them in this way, through professors who believe an evangelical woman, with experience in the city, needs to be a voice among the many liberal voices who are shaping the direction of urban mission. He affirmed me through providing the finances at just the right time, and through powerful notes of thanks from persons in the city...I could go on and on.

Am I still afraid of these new challenges? Do I still fight God at times? Yes, I do. But, my prayer is that I will not only know about God, or pray to him in times of trouble, or even obey God—I want to trust him with my whole heart so he can make my heart like his own. When my experiences of mercy, comfort, hope, and love overflow in healing, mercy and transformation for others, then there is salvation for both me and my friends in the city.

In closing, remember I said earlier that I believed Jonah's heart also changed. The sad thing we learn from the Bible and history is that Israel's heart did not change. In fact, during the next generation, God used Nineveh and the Assyrians, the very people who did repent, to judge the people of Israel who did not repent.

We, as God's people, cannot take lightly the message of Jonah—God wants our hearts to be like his own. Only then will our obedience, our prayers, and our knowledge of him result in the kind of intimacy with God and love for others, in the kind of God-likeness, that brings healing and blessing to others. Only then will God's mercy to us overflow in mercy to others.

GUDRUN MATTIES

The Earth is a House for All People

Psalm 8

Psalm 8 begins and ends with the refrain, "O Lord, Our Lord, how majestic is your name in all the earth!" and goes on to say "You made him ruler over the works of your hands, you put everything under his feet."

The temptation is to treat the earth as if it were our own possession rather than as God's gift for all humanity to cherish and tentatively hold.

God sees people as part of the same family and the earth as the house for all people. If we acknowledge that God is the creator and sustainer of all creation, then we are bound to honor God through our daily relationships in respect for the world that God has created.

How seriously do we individually and as a church body take the admonition to be earthkeepers? As faithful Christians we dare not isolate ourselves from the concerns of the rest of the world. When we think globally we may be paralyzed by the immensity of the task. We may easily be overwhelmed by events that seem out of control —war, violence, famine and environmental destruction.

Our prayers need to be accompanied by some tangible actions. However, the need must be small enough that we can relate significantly to it or we will dismiss it as an impossibility.

We may doubt as the disciples did at the feeding of the 5000, that five loaves and two fish were adequate for the hungry crowd. But the combination of each individual effort can make a difference. There are many examples and signs of this kind of hope.

Jean Vanier, who has lived for 30 years with mentally and physically challenged people, once decided to offer a home to two of these persons in a small French village. Today all over the world, as a result of that caring action, L'Arche communities offer safe havens for mentally challenged persons.

What conditions would we like to see completely forgotten in a new order? How will God's promises make life on earth radically different for people in all parts of the world? What radical role could we plan to bring hope, justice and peace to a hurting world as we wait for God's new heaven and new earth?

SYLVIA M. KLAUSER

Holding On to the Promise

Isaiah

I used to like reading the promises given to Isaiah and his prophet friends. I liked those promises that pointed towards the coming of the Messiah. But even more than reading the words, I love to listen to the music and the words of the oratorio composed by Handel. And it does not make any difference if it is the soul version these days, the poetic promises are still the same. It almost seems that the combination of music and words are touching the deepest strings of the soul.

Even though we are reading the words of the promise, sometimes it feels empty; it makes no sense. The strings of our soul are out of tune. Every musician knows that there is nothing worse than an instrument that is out of tune. And every Christian knows that life is not fun when the soul is out of tune. When I accepted this opportunity to preach, my soul sounded pretty horrible because my emotional and spiritual strings were out of tune (they still are to a certain extent). But God has great ways to get us places and to let us experience things. For me it was the topic of the sermon; **Holding on to the Promise** that kept me intrigued. So, reluctantly, I turned to Isaiah, once my favorite prophet.

When the dissonance of my soul was at its worst, I found Philip Yancy's book *Disappointed with God* (HarperPaperbacks. New York. 1988). Now you might ask, what do promises and disappointment have to do with each other? More than one sees at first glance. Yancey tries to answer the questions, "Is God silent? Is God unfair? Is God hidden?" by looking at the biblical text from Genesis to Revelation for answers. In the section about the prophets he said something that turned my whole understanding of promises, prophets, the birth of Christ, and Handel's famous musical interpretation upside-down.

Before I go any further, I want to highlight one crucial point that needs to be considered when reading God's word. When we read the Bible we tend to read in retrospect. So, when we read the promise about Abraham becoming a great nation, with as many people as the stars in the sky, our brains race through history and biblical narrative from the past to present time. A second later something in us says that the promise is true, it is a great nation. Not so for Abraham. He sat there in the desert with his mobile farm and looked around for a long time to find this son who was to be the proof for the promise. He didn't find him for the longest time. He had only the promise and no Bible to tell him how the story would turn out. When the prophets were proclaiming all the great promises to the people of Israel, they had no clue how long it would take to the fulfillment.

Four hundred years of silence, deafening silence, twice as long as the existence of this country. Nothing but silence and some promises to hang on to, spouted out by a few weirdoes called prophets. Generation after generation tried to keep up with those promises but the political climate was too tense, the prospect of captivity in Babylon too real in order to understand Isaiah's promise in chapter 9 verses 2,3,6,7.

> *The people walking in darkness have seen a great light; on those living in the land of the shadow of death a light has dawned. You have enlarged the nation and increased their joy; they rejoice before you as people rejoice at the harvest, as men rejoice when dividing the plunder. For to us a child is born, to us a son is given, and the government will be on his shoulders. And he will be called Wonderful Counselor, Mighty God, Everlasting Father, Prince of Peace. Of the increase of his government and peace there will be no end. He will reign on David's throne and over his kingdom, establishing and upholding it with justice and righteousness from that time on and forever. The zeal of the LORD Almighty will accomplish this.*

What is Isaiah talking about? Which son is reigning on David's throne? Why is it that the zeal of the Lord Almighty does not do much these days? These or similar questions were likely being asked by the people of Israel. Micah, a contemporary of Isaiah, even knew where this new king was supposed to be coming from. Micah

5:2 says, *"But you, Bethlehem Ephrathah, though you are small among the clans of Judah, out of you will come for me one who will be ruler over Israel, whose origins are from of old, from ancient times."* But this promise did not seem to be too impressive either for the Israelites, in the light of the upcoming move eastwards to Babylon. In the next 200 plus years, the chosen people of God did not care a great deal about the promises. Life was too tough with all the adjustments to the new culture, making money and surviving, doing a good job and prospering, just as Jeremiah told them to do. There was neither room nor need to hang on too tightly to the promise. Later, when the people of Israel felt the wind of change again, when the kingdom of Babylon began to crumble, Isaiah had a new promise to bring them hope (Isaiah 40:1-5, 9-11).

"Isaiah, what does it mean? We are still here in an alien land, Jerusalem is still demolished, and we still don't get it!" Do you sometimes feel that you don't get the idea of the promises? I certainly feel that way. For Israel, these words of the prophet did not make any sense, their souls were out of tune. But some were hanging on to the promise anyway. What could they lose? Then when they finally got home from exile and started building up the city, Isaiah spoke again.

> *Arise, shine, for your light has come, and the glory of the LORD rises upon you. See, darkness covers the earth and thick darkness is over the peoples, but the LORD rises upon you and his glory appears over you. Nations will come to your light, and kings to the brightness of your dawn. (Isaiah 60:1-3)*

"Prophet, why don't you get the picture here? There is no Messiah, no light, no glory of the

Lord. All there is, is occupation by the enemy, no material to work with, no land to grow food, nothing but depression, even in freedom. And what light are you talking about?" Their souls were out of tune and only a handful of people were barely hanging on to the promise. A few more years and a few minor prophets later the silence fell. God did not speak anymore. All that was left were the promises handed down from generation to generation by means of story. No e-mail or newspaper, no CNN, NBC or CBS. Just plain stories about some promises of a silent God. Waiting and silence.

Advent is the time of waiting for the Messiah. It is the time of preparing ourselves to welcome the prince of peace. Joy overflows, we can hardly wait for Christmas Eve, the gifts and "Silent Night, Holy Night." The alternative reading of the Christmas story suggests though that while we are dancing with joy, God is hiding his face, stricken with tears. His heart is aching with almost unbearable pain over the last resources he has - giving up his beloved son to bridge the gap to his creation. Imagine the worst emotional pain you have felt in your life - this is what God feels. Because he loves us and because of the promise he gave Noah to never again destroy all living creatures, because he was courting a people who did not understand this kind of God, because of the sum total of history he had to give up Jesus to be true to his promises.

My first point of challenge for this Advent season is to think about God, the father and lover, think about what it cost him and what it must have felt like to give up his dearest and only Son.

My second challenge has to do with the way we treat Advent. Because we read the promises in retrospect, because we listen to Handel's Messiah from a different historical viewpoint, because we know how the story ends, we have developed uncountable techniques to lessen the silence and make the waiting less boring. And we're hanging on to the promise that the Messiah will come and something will change, even if the only changes are the types of activities we go through during a given Advent season. Concerts, shopping, eating; shopping, concerts, eating; eating, shopping, concerts - you get the idea? Oh yes, and hanging on to the promise. While reading and thinking about this sermon, I found that we actually are not such distant relatives to the Israelites. While we don't have to wait 400 years for the fulfillment of the promise of Christmas, our 28 days seem even harder to learn from. We have more distractions to shorten the time of waiting.

While I was going through my time of barely hanging on to the promises, the time when I didn't understand what was happening, I was talking to one of my professors. He gave me some advice that I'm not sure I can follow. He said to just take the uncertainty and silence, the boring pain of screaming silence, and just hold it in my hand, to just let it sit there for a while, to wait for what will develop out of it. This advice goes 100% against my German work ethic of productivity and success. Since I share this heritage with some of you, maybe you can relate to my hesitations. Just waiting and holding the promise until the light comes seems an impossible task. Imagine the Israelites during the 400 years of God's silence. They had no Bible to read when life got rough, they couldn't look back at the hero stories the way we can, and they certainly couldn't look ahead to understand like we can with the help of the Holy Spirit. All they could do was "hang in there" and wait for the promises to be fulfilled.

I want to challenge us at the beginning of this Advent season to take the time to sit and wait for the promise to be fulfilled in whatever personal way that might be for each of us. It is very easy to lessen the silence but Advent is certainly too precious for just concerts, eating and shopping. Last week we heard that our only legitimate response to God's word is the obedience and perseverance which will result in true regeneration. My prayer is that during this Advent season we will be able to be fruitful soils for God's promises to grow in us and that we can regenerate so much that our life will make a difference in the world. Let us take time to respond to God as we take time to reflect on the fulfillment of God's promises in each of our lives.

TIFFANY FRIESEN

The One Who Is Faithful to the Faithful One

Luke 1:39-56

The text found in Luke 1:39-56 is one we often use at Christmas because of its location in the nativity story. We read Mary's hymn of praise, the Magnificat, specifically on Mary's Sunday in Advent to consider the favor God showed to Mary. At other times, we use it as a guide for understanding the way God will deal with the rich and mighty, and raise up the poor and the lowly. Today, however, I would like us to focus on Mary's understanding of who she is, her view of herself in relationship to God and to others, and her obedience to her Savior, who is God. I would like to suggest that we look, in light of this text, at the person and life of Mary and the inspiration she is to our faith.

In Luke 1 Mary speaks to us from her own experience. We know very little about Mary except that she was a woman from Nazareth who was engaged to a man named Joseph. An angel appeared to her announcing that the Lord had found favor with her and she would bear a son and name him Jesus. She counts herself among the humble and the poor. She has encountered the mystery and power of the Holy Spirit; first upon conception and now as she emotes words of praise and adoration for her Savior God. Without seeing or touching God, she gives her body, will, intellect, and emotions to God's purpose. Prior to receiving the message from the angel, she probably had a much different life in mind for herself. Never would she have planned to be ridiculed by her community for being pregnant before being married, or having a son who runs away to the temple and leaves her worrying for three days. She would never have imagined that "a sword would pierce her very soul" as she watched the child she birthed be crucified on a cross. But she acknowledged God's way and drew comfort and trust from it. She is an example of one who grasped the incomprehensible through faith. Mary had faith in the promise of God and she acted on it.

Mary also remembers the promises God made to the people in the land of Israel and recognizes that now is the time of fulfillment. Throughout all of history that has passed and is yet to come, God has chosen to fulfill this promise of his Son now, with the help of Mary. She knows that God is mighty, that she is lowly and that God has chosen her. She is not ignorant in her faith. She is a humble and willing hostess to the greatest guest of all.

Mary is not only convinced of God's power in the past and present but also for the future. She is so sure of God's just dealings with the mighty and the lowly in future generations that she speaks the last part of her hymn in the past tense.

> *He has performed mighty deeds with his arm;*
> *he has scattered those who are proud in their*
> *inmost thoughts. He has brought down rulers*
> *from their thrones but has lifted up the hum-*
> *ble. He has filled the hungry with good things*
> *but has sent the rich away empty. He has*
> *helped his servant Israel, remembering to be*
> *merciful to Abraham and his descendants for-*
> *ever, even as he said to our fathers. (vv. 51-55)*

Mary's heritage in God and her tradition of faith have given her assurance that God's people will not be forsaken. God has made promises and covenants with his people and has never forgotten them. He has remembered Mary, a humble bondslave and shown mercy to future generations by sending his son. Why then would God not continue to intervene in the lives of his people forever? Only God can scatter the proud in heart, bring down rulers, exalt the humble, fill the hungry with food and send the rich away empty handed. Only God can achieve a just society in the last days. The God of Mary is the God of Abraham, Miriam, Hannah, David, and Job. He is the God of the past, the present and the future. It is this God who has blessed her womb and to whom she sings a hymn of praise.

Mary gives birth to the Christ child, nurtures him and watches him grow. But it is none of this that makes her a saint. In fact, all the while Joseph and Mary were raising a son, this son, Jesus, was receiving training and guidance from his true father in heaven. Mary's family ties to Jesus do not come only from her physical motherhood. They also come from her faith in the one true God. Although Mary watched Jesus grow up, teach, be mocked and killed, her faith was not shaken. In fact, Luke places her both in Jesus' pre- and post-Easter community. She is at the cross and in the upper room praying with the other disciples, waiting to receive the Holy Spirit. Mary is a woman of faith, a disciple of Christ who believed what was spoken to her.

As has been stated many times, Mary's faithfulness made her blessed. Mary's faith was in the God she called Savior; the one who had acted faithfully in the past and had blessed her life with a miraculous child. A child who was ultimately the Earth's Messiah, the one in whom all could receive mercy. Mary's faithfulness is a model for us in a number of ways.

Mary continually had her focus upon God her Savior. God her Savior. I had to stop and think about this phrase. I do not usually think of the phrase "God is my Savior." For some reason or another the phrase most common in my mind has been of "Jesus Christ my Savior." The story of Mary and her Magnificat has helped me to view the story of God and his people in a new light. Ultimately the story of the Bible is an account of God intervening in the lives of people. God is the initiator of covenants. God makes the promises. God keeps the promises. God is constantly drawing us into closer fellowship with himself. The ultimate connection that God makes with the world is the sending of Jesus Christ to live on earth. But even Christ, through his teachings, hearings, and miracles commands that all glory and recognition be given to God the Father. It is through Jesus (and only him) that we can have a clearer sense of who God is. It is God who desires to be a part of our lives.

Another witness of faith is Mary's song to God. In it she mentions the people of God in the past, herself, the mighty and the humble, and future generations. All of these have an effect on the way she views God. God has intervened in the lives of all these people. God has remembered her, has blessed the poor and fed the hungry. God has done mighty deeds with his arm. Then she mentions her past and the people of her faith tradition. She remembers that God has done right by them and has fulfilled his promises. It is in her acknowledgment of God's past actions that I find the most comfort. Mary did not hear the voice of an unknown God. She did not whimsically choose to obey. She knew enough about the nature of the God who called her, to know that giving herself to him was the only reasonable thing to do. She had no idea of the details that would follow. She did not know exactly what her son would be like, what he would do or that he would die a painful death. What she did know was that God was faithful.

I want to be more like Mary. When God requests that I go somewhere or do something other than what I have planned, I want to remember that this is not a foreign voice. I want the kind of faith that looks to God as my Savior and recognizes him as sovereign in my life. I want to sing songs of praise to God, be obedient to his will, and believe in him to such a degree that my friends, coworkers and someday, future generations can say they believe in my God.

As a community of faith I call us to remember this God who has guided the people of our past.

I call us to remember that the same God who has been the Savior of our past is (and to use Mary's language, has been) the Savior of the future. We can have confidence that God will remember us, will provide food for the hungry, and lift up the humble. God will deal justly with the proud and the mighty.

Most importantly I believe that as a community of faith it is our joy to remind each other of the ways God has worked in our lives in the past. We then remind each other that God is here now and will remain in our lives in the future. God will and does continually choose to intervene in our lives, constantly drawing us into a closer relationship with himself.

I encourage each one of us to make a conscious effort to notice the way God has been a part of our lives. At the day's end, think back on your day and notice how God has been near. At the end of the week, take time to thank God for his presence. Look around too, at the people with whom you are in contact; your family, your colleagues, your small fellowship groups, and remind them of the ways God has been making himself known to you. Also, let them know you have seen God at work in their lives. If you stop to reflect on these times and ponder them in your heart like Mary, I guarantee your soul will swell with praises. And when this happens, grab a pencil and paper or a keyboard and write your own MAGNIFICAT.

ELFRIEDA NIKKEL

A Time of Encouragement

Christmas has been a time of encouragement to many over the years. It is the time when we try to express love and goodwill to family and friends. Even our routine business trips to the grocery store or the bank are sprinkled with well wishes for the Christmas season.

A special part of the Christmas story is Mary's visit to Elizabeth. What beautiful words of encouragement and affirmation are spoken by Elizabeth. Mary's response to this encouragement, "My soul magnifies the Lord..." has been a rich blessing to Christians over the centuries. Words of encouragement are like a ripple in the water. They have a way of rolling on and on, from one person to another.

Who are the "Mary's" that come to us for encouragement? Can we be as kind and generous with our words as Elizabeth was? We may never know the far reaching results of the words we speak as we seek to encourage others on the road of life.

VANGE THIESSEN

The Kind Of Dad Kids Come Back To

Luke 15:11-31

The germ of this sermon has evolved from within my own experience this past year. In an Old Testament theology class last fall at Mennonite Brethren Biblical Seminary we discussed the roles of men and women. Certainly no point of agreement was reached. The next morning after everyone had left the house and it was my turn for the shower, I began to sense a feeling of loss. At first the tears were confusing, then I seemed to get in touch with the loss of a father who was "there but not there." The very roles which the church supported took my father away from a relational connectedness with his family. I became angry. The role of provider, his position as head of the house, his place of control and power deeply impacted our family relationships. The trauma of unresolved conflict contributed to the premature leaving of several older brothers. It was only in his later years that the sensitivity and tenderness of his true character began to surface. He died in 1981. In our family only some of the kids (now middle-aged) came back.

The Kind of Dad Kids Come Back to

The text as heard in story form, is the parable we most commonly know as the "Prodigal Son."

Various commentators give alternate titles such as the "Parable of the Lost Son" or recognizing it as a two-peaked narrative it has also been named the "Parable of the Two Sons." Yet another suggestion follows the idea that the father is indeed the central character of the story thus calling it the "Parable of a Father's Love." It is the image of the father in the story that I wish to highlight today.

The commentators seems to agree that the father is a symbol of God. The characteristics and attitudes of a loving heavenly Father are portrayed in this. This parable further provides a prototype or example of God the parent responding to his/her children. While I understand the image of God as parent to be inclusive of both male and female characteristics, I am choosing to use male-father language today since I am specifically addressing the men and fathers in this sermon. What is it about this father that makes it possible for kids to come back?

The Kind of Dad Kids Come Back to Grants Permission to Leave

The story begins, "There was once a man who had two sons." The man is presumably a Palestinian Jewish farmer or landowner who is relatively well off. The younger son in one of his bolder moments comes to the father and requests his share of the estate. In the culture of that day the younger son's share would have been one-third of the estate, since the elder was allotted a double portion. It still seems a ludicrous request, does it not? Imagine yourself in the place of this father. The family farm, business or vocation has been passed down from generation to generation. Your own struggle to follow in the family tradition, in time, creates a strong loyalty and commitment to the task. Over the years you have sacrificed in order for your children to gain a better education, a better start in life. And now this! Your son at age 18 wants his share of the inheritance. But what does he know about wise investments? How can you let him go on his own? Do you not feel an obligation to teach him the ways of the world? Thinking of all your mistakes in the past, you wish you could prevent his fall.

Again the request comes, a response is required. Contrary to what many parents today would consider a wise and prudent choice, the father obliges. Though various authors comment on the rebellious or disobedient nature of the younger son, I do not see it in the text. The plan of action appears purposeful and intentional. Separation from the parental home is accomplished by a distinct physical removal to a "distant land." No longer under the watchful eye of his father, the son is able to live without restraint and accountability.

But it is more than a physical leaving. In that day the command to honor parents was understood concretely as the responsibility to care for them in old age. By his actions the younger son also severed emotional relations with his father. He denied his status as son by cutting the ties of love and care.

What kind of father would give permission for a son to leave under such conditions? What merit is there in letting go? Is not the risk too great? There is no evidence in the narrative of a conflictual battle between father and son. And yet I can't imagine it was an easy separation. What might a father experience? Again try to put yourself in his place—would you feel loss, anger, pain, fear, disappointment?

For many parents this may be the most difficult aspect of parenting—letting go! This same struggle is depicted in the relationship of God and Israel. The metaphor of child and loving father is used. Listen to these words:

> *When Israel was a child, I loved him, and out of Egypt I called my son. It was I who taught Ephraim to walk, taking him by the arms; I led them with cords of human kindness, with ties of love; I lifted the yoke from their neck and bent down to feed them. But the more I called Israel the further they went from me. They did not realize it was I who healed them. How can I give you up, Ephraim? How can I hand you over, Israel? My heart is changed within me; all my compassion is aroused. I will not carry out my fierce anger, nor devastate Ephraim again. They will come back trembling....I will settle them in their homes. (Hosea 11: 1-4, 8-11)*

In order for his child to come back, the father first gives the son permission to leave.

The Kind of Dad Kids Come Back to Maintains an Open Relationship of Waiting and Watching

Separations are often so difficult in relationships that one or both of the parties tends to move toward cut-off. Physical and ideological distancing may also lead to emotional distance. The cost of non-conformity in many Mennonite households has tragically ended in broken relationships.

Being the youngest of nine children, only now am I hearing how several of my older brothers left home in willful defiance while feeling shamed and hurt on the inside. They perceived my father to be distant, authoritarian and interested only in the things of the church. In contrast I remember the time we shared shortly before my father's death. We had returned from Kentucky and Melissa, just three years old, loved to crawl on his lap and comb his hair down over his eyes and then back again. It could have been experienced as an annoying gesture and certainly a waste of time, but he sat there patiently indulging her preference and perhaps even quietly enjoying those intimate moments with his granddaughter.

Just as the child begins to separate and explore the world beyond, an inner alarm seems to trigger the child's need for reassurance. The child needs a secure place to come back to. This is often very confusing for parents. How can one honestly remain there for the child when they are pushing so hard against everything one stands for. These critical points tend to occur during the toddler stage, in adolescence and if not sufficiently resolved, again in mid-life. I have encountered numerous adults in parenting classes who struggle with their family of origin issues when their own children reach pre-adolescence. How do we hold together the need both to separate and to be connected?

The father remains ever hopeful, waiting, perhaps daily searching the distant horizon for his son's reappearance. He believed his son would come back. The meeting was no mere acknowledgment. It was filled with exuberance and compassion. The Greek word for *compassion* means "to have the bowels yearning." I like that, rather earthy isn't it? It signifies a deep, inner response of affection and tender mercy. Some comment that a father in that culture would not normally run as he did, which along with his embrace and kissing breaks traditional customs. I wonder if that has changed in our culture?

The qualities of care, nurture, receptivity, emotion, and self-sacrifice have been designated as feminine and frequently are devalued in our society. In my own conversations with men, however, rejection of masculine stereotypes seems more common. This is also becoming a visible topic in the field of marriage and family therapy. Last fall a marriage and family therapy conference included three plenary speakers who addressed men's issues of sexuality, commitment and father-son relationships. A recent family journal focuses on men nurturing men. Something very refreshing is happening out there. Could it be that Biblical truth is being discovered outside the organized church while inside its walls we tenaciously hold on to traditional patterns?

Frank Pittman tells his own story. "I was not a football-playing brute at a time and place when that was the masculine ideal, and the model my father had given me. I never thought I was masculine enough for him. Back in my 20s and 30s, I was still impressed with men who seemed more masculine that I, who were richer and controlled more things and people. ... (Even after I married) I still felt I wasn't masculine enough, and when we had a son, I was afraid I couldn't be the man he needed as a father ... (Wherever I turned in my profession as a therapist, I found men who feared they were not masculine enough) ... My father — the warrior, the athlete, the boss of the town ... loved me as his boy but had never affirmed me as a man. As he was dying, I talked a lot about manhood with my son, who was 18, a champion athlete, and a strong man in the mold of his grandfather. My son and I could affirm one another. We laughed and cried over being one another's hero and that gave me the courage to finally talk with my stern, silent father about how I saw him and how he saw me ... Once I knew he saw me as a man I could hug him, for the first time ... I try to remember how old I was before I could hug a male friend, and how sad I was that it took me so long, but I could never hug my father until he was dying."(Frank Pittman. The Male Mystique. *Family Therapy Networker.* May/June 1990, p.51)

Deborah Luepnitz identifies a feminist therapy which includes a passionate plea for making families less patriarchal and less father absent. The task is to bring fathers closer to the heart of child care; a father who will not be the tired nightly visitor, rather one who is an authentic presence, a tender and engaged parent, a knower of children. Recent research links the ability to separate and the formation of empathy in a child to father involvement with preschool children.

The response of compassion in the parable is followed by an act of charity. It is not sufficient to point out that the father's welcome was filled with emotion and feeling. The behavior or action which followed was congruent with the emotion and demonstrated his acceptance in a tangible way. The symbols of a ring and coat reinstated his sonship.

For the son, the remembrance of his father's open relationship no doubt facilitated his decision to return home.

The Kind of Dad Kids Come Back to Takes the Initiative to Seek Out

Amidst the celebration and festivities the father never loses sight of an obvious vacancy. The father leaves the party in search of his elder son. The use of the term *entreated* in Greek conveys the meaning "to come alongside, to comfort and exhort." When he finds him, the son's feelings of jealousy, anger, resentment and perhaps insecurity begin to pour out. All these years he has worked to earn a place in the family and yet he perceives a great distance. The father's initiative shows sensitivity, understanding, and unconditional love.

I think it is noteworthy to point out that though the elder son had never left home, his absence from the celebration showed his distant relationship from the family. But had he not complied and followed all the rules? Yet the father was not deceived. The elder son was as much in need of his love and mercy as was the younger. Right knowledge and right behavior were not sufficient to bring about a sense of belonging. In fact it is often our "good children" that are most in need of the message of grace. Sensing a need to perform and earn their place in the family, they often fail to understand the concept of "gift" in a father's relationship of love.

Think for a moment about the powerful nurturing force of getting there first. How often as a parent do we wait for our children to come to us? That's the way it was at our house. As a child I remember begging for those summer vacations. When father finally gave in it seemed a hollow victory. Somehow it never quite felt like a gift. What a different feeling when I received those dozen roses from my family right after graduation—I hadn't even asked for them!

A friend of mine shared this incident. For

weeks he responded to his daughter's nightly call to tuck her into bed. Before he left the room she would always say, "I love you Daddy." He then would echo, "I love you too, Tamara." One night she broke the pattern, "I wish you had said that first, Daddy."

The father, in the case of the elder son got there first. He took the initiative to seek and to come alongside.

The Kind of Dad Kids Come Back to Possesses the Ability to Celebrate

The statement, "We had to celebrate and be glad" seems to refer to something larger than the younger brother's physical return. The joy over the lost being found is a common theme in the three parables of the lost sheep, the coin, and the son. While the father rejoices that his younger son is found and alive, he longs to be inclusive in the celebration and thus he extends the invitation to the elder son. The feast is a celebration of reconciled relationships.

Jean Vanier has some wonderful things to say about celebration. "To love someone is not to do something for them, but to rejoice in their existence. Forgiveness and celebration are at the heart of community. These are the two faces of love." (Faith and Sharing Retreat, Victoria, BC, 1989) Fathers, when you reveal to a child how happy you are that they exist, the process of trust is initiated. Celebration nourishes us, it restores hope and brings strength to live with the disappointments, the suffering and difficulties of everyday life.

In summary, the characteristics in this parable of a Father's love are: (1) He gives permission to leave without imposing his personal expectations. (2) Throughout the separation he watches and awaits the younger son's return all the while maintaining an open, tender, hopeful and affectionate relationship. (3) Not only is he available, but he takes the initiative to seek out the elder son. As he comes alongside he shows sensitivity and understanding to the questions, the resentments, the hostilities, the needs and the desires of his child. (4) Finally he celebrates the joy of finding and reconciling broken relationships, the discovery of true connectedness between father and son, between father and daughter.

As men, as fathers, I hope that your eyes continue to see more of God as the loving, nurturing, faithful parent. Amen.

CONNIE EPP

God as Mother?

Luke 15:11-31 NRSV

Over a dozen years ago I gave birth to the most incredible baby boy that I have ever seen. Amazing. Gorgeous. Miraculous. Wow! What a gift Ken and I had been given! He was a brand new writhing, wriggling, squeaking little life that pulled emotions and sensations out of me that didn't match any single experience of the past. I thought I knew what love was but this was a whole new dimension. I was instantly aware that I would do anything for the good of this child. I would give everything for the good of this child. He would be forevermore a part of me. That experience was repeated three years later with our daughter's birth.

In Isaiah 49:15 God asks, *"Can a woman forget her nursing child, or show no compassion for the child of her womb?"* Then it goes on to say, *"Even these may forget, yet I will not forget you."*

I respond, "God, are you saying that your love is even greater than my love for my children? You have chosen to use one of the strongest human examples of love and devotion and now you're telling me that your love goes even beyond that? I can't fathom what that must be like. How can you possibly love more?"

God replies, "I do."

My mother knew everything about me. I think she had some kind of secret antenna, not to mention eyes in the back of her head. She seemed to know what was going on in my life even when she wasn't with me. When we'd get home from church, for example, she would know whom I sat with, how much we talked or laughed, where we sat and whom we disturbed. She could even predict where I would be sitting next week!!

While her intimate knowledge of me was at times annoying, it also comforted me when she knew what a particular problem was even though I couldn't verbalize it. I knew she cared enough to know - to take an interest in my life.

I think of my mother when I read Psalm 139. *"You know when I sit down and when I rise up; you discern my thoughts from far away. You ... are acquainted with all my ways. Even before a word is on my tongue ... you know it completely"* (vv. 2-4).

Again I respond, "You care about me that much, God? You know everything I do and think and feel? It's all relevant to you? How can you do that for me when you have so many children? How can I be important enough? I can't fathom what that's like. Do you love me that much?"

God replies, "I do."

God is always too much to fathom. We can never know God completely. But we have been given clues to help us come closer to understanding. The Bible is packed full of incredible imagery that tells us what God is like. These pictures - parallels to our own lives - help us to focus a little better and bring us closer to the truth.

If we were told only that "God is God" we would have no idea of what that meant. The gap between ourselves and God would be too great. Incomprehensible! But the Bible contains incredible illustrations for our benefit.

God is described as many things some of which are shepherd, righteous judge, lion, lioness, shield, rock, mother hen, refuge, king, lamb, father, mother, and there are many, many more.

It is interesting to note that there appear to be some contradictions in that list. How can a shepherd also be a lamb? How can a lion be a lioness? How can a king be a mother hen? How can a father also be a mother?

Hosea 11:9 gives us a clue, *"For I am God and no mortal, the Holy One in your midst."* God seems to be saying, "You cannot confine me to these images, people. I am so much more. I have given these pictures to you for your benefit - so you can have a small glimpse of who I really am." The Bible describes what God is like but it cannot ever completely say what God actually is. There are no words or images that are ever comprehensive enough to provide us with a total picture.

The fact is, though, that we choose some pictures over others. We give priority to illustrations that best match what we want God to be. We prefer images of might and power. Page through most church hymn books and see which images are the most popular: King, Father, Almighty One. We still seem to want the same Messiah that the Jews were hoping for. Lambs, mothers, and hens aren't nearly as popular. They just don't project the right image. But then neither do donkeys, yet Jesus chose to enter Jerusalem on a donkey instead of on a king's noble steed.

Did God give us these metaphors so we could decide which would be our favorites and which we would exclude? I don't think so. Not only do these images give us clues as to who and what God is, but by relating our experiences to God, they in turn also validate who and what we and God's entire creation are.

Take God as shepherd, for example. We're not talking about your average Christmas pageant shepherds in their cozy velour housecoats who just had their Christmas bath before they came to church. No, we're talking about grungy, smelly, illiterate, rough and tumble guys that sleep on rocks, who have the innate ability to scare off wolves or bears and who communicate primarily with sheep. These guys were considered to be the lowest of the low, bottom of the social scale. And yet God says, "I am the good shepherd." Can you imagine...God compared to these sheepsitters? Yet God chooses to give us this image as an example. Imagine what this example does for the shepherd.

But God is also called king, the opposite extreme. In these two images God gives us the whole spectrum. God relates to each end - king and shepherd. So why do we choose to focus primarily on the image of power? Take another look at typical church music or the passages we choose to emphasize in our worship services and count the kings compared to the shepherds.

But shepherds actually hold their own quite well in comparison to mothers or for that matter any kind of female or feminine imagery. How many mother hymns come to mind? Yet we have been given much female and feminine imagery in both the Old and the New Testaments. By female imagery I am referring to aspects of life that are unique to women such as childbirth. Women can give birth. Men cannot.

Female imagery says, "Yes, women and women's experiences are valid." In the book of Isaiah God says, *"For a long time I have held my peace, I have kept still and restrained myself; now I will cry out like a woman in labor, I will gasp and pant" (42:14)*. When I hear that, I share the frustration and intensity God went through. It echoes my own experience. God has chosen to relate very personally to me through this aspect of my life. God has selected an experience that is not common to the whole world. It is like a personal touchpoint that tells me that in God's eyes my life and experiences are valid too.

By feminine imagery, as compared to female imagery, I am referring to traits that have generally been associated with women (such as nurturing, compassion, and caring) but that are accessible to men as well. Men can choose to love and care just as women can choose to love and care. Feminine imagery validates feminine virtues for the whole community. The scriptures tell us that loving, caring, and nurturing are all important. Women have been the primary caregivers but these are important qualities for the community as a whole to express and experience.

Jesus modeled for us the traits that our society in general sees as less important, as feminine. He was sensitive, nurturing, compassionate. He saw the person, not the position. People were always a priority. Status, power, and self interest were not.

I am not saying that God is a woman. But God is also not a man. God became flesh, in the form of a man, but before God became flesh, God was obviously not flesh or not human. God says, *"For I am God and no mortal, the Holy One in your midst" (Hosea 11:9)*. By encouraging involvement of both males and females in all aspects of church life, we are benefiting from what each has to offer. We are allowing the Holy Spirit to move freely among all of us regardless of gender. We are being exposed to a more complete, well-rounded picture instead of just the masculine side of the image that has been predominant in the past. People and caring ministries are increasingly in the forefront. We are coming to realize how important these aspects of our faith walk are. Feminine qualities are being recognized as valid and vital. We are beginning to achieve balance.

I think God had balance in mind when we were given these many illustrations. By focusing only on a select few we lose out. By pushing some too far forward or too far back we may miss the point. And by pushing them back and forth, we push people with them. When we think we are insulting God by saying "mother," for example, are we implying that women are inferior and God needs to be referred to as a male to preserve dignity? Is it okay to call God a rock, but not a mother? What does that say to the mothers in our midst?

We must work together as God's community to continually search for truth and justice. Searching is hard work. Our walk can never be static. We must be open to teaching, exploring, discovering, and questioning in order to let God work in us and through us. We must learn to know God intimately. And as we come to know God better, we will realize the picture enlarges and becomes more excitingly complex instead of smaller and predictably clearer. And as that picture enlarges, we come to realize how limiting any one name is for God. God will not be confined to king, rock, father, shepherd, or mother. We see a part of God in all these images and yet God is much more than any or all of these.

J.B.Phillips' book, *Your God is Too Small* (1987), suggests perhaps we are guilty of diminishing God. Maybe it's easier for us to maintain control when God is restricted to the confines of our understanding. Deuteronomy 4:15-18 says:

> *Since you saw no form when the Lord spoke to you at Horeb out of the fire, take care and watch yourselves closely, so that you do not act corruptly by making an idol for yourselves, in the form of any figure - the likeness of male or female, the likeness of any animal that is on the earth, the likeness of any winged bird that flies in the air, the likeness of anything that creeps on the ground, the likeness of any fish that is in the water under the earth.*

When we continually focus on only a few images and cast others aside, are we not guilty of this idolatry?

Theologian Herbert Richardson recalls being taught a bedtime prayer that he recited throughout childhood. It began, "Father-Mother God, loving me." (Sally McFague. *Models of God: Theology for an Ecological, Nuclear Age.* Fortress Press, 1987, p.97) He said it impressed upon his young mind that if God was both father and mother, then God was much more than anything else he knew.

Most of us have grown up calling God Father. We have many examples of father imagery. Father is good. But have we lost another whole dimension of who God is? Have we also, then, by doing so, trivialized or invalidated those who were made in that lost part of the image of God? Have we actually formed God into our own desired image to the point where we consider it sin if we call God anything beyond father and king?

This is not an easy issue for many of us but we dare not simply accept something just because it's been done in the past. Tradition can offer much but we must continually examine it under the microscope of truth and justice. We have to search it out for ourselves. We must read, pray, discern and open ourselves to God's guidance.

> *Ask, and it will be given you; search, and you will find; knock, and the door will be opened for you. For everyone who asks receives, and everyone who searches finds, and for everyone who knocks, the door will be opened. (Matthew 7:7,8)*

God, guide us in our quest.

HEDY LEONORA MARTENS

Begotten of God

1 John 5:1-6 NRSV

Could we bow our heads and think for a moment about God, the Father of our Lord Jesus Christ? Could we imagine that we can see the far-flung galaxies of God's creation — the worlds upon worlds? Could we add to that all of those invisible worlds which "no eye has seen, nor ear heard, and of which even our hearts have not yet been able to conceive"? (I Cor. 2:9) In awe, let us acknowledge that we speak to One who is beyond our comprehension. In gratitude, let us offer up our thanks.

According to the book, *The Community of the Beloved Disciple* (Raymond E. Brown, 1979), 1 John was a letter written to the community that had been born because of the witness of "the beloved disciple" mentioned in the Gospel of John. Therefore, the people in this community were steeped in this Gospel, with its emphasis on the preexistence of Christ and the love of God which sent him to earth. They resonated with its images of water, light, and new birth. They were convinced that all — even Gentiles and Samaritans— could worship God in Spirit and in truth, for the Spirit had come, and had led them into truth, as Jesus had promised. But sadly, now that "the beloved disciple" himself is no longer among them, disagreements have splintered this community. Some have already left, pursuing other more extreme interpretations of the Gospel. Those who remain are confused, frightened, and probably divided. The letter of 1 John is sent into that confusion and into that fear.

The Gospel of John lent itself to such misinterpretation because it was written to counter the belief that Jesus was only human, not divine. So it stressed Christ's preexistence, and played down his humanity. But both were present, and this is what the writer of 1 John builds on.

For example, during the writing of the gospel the rabbis taught that God was at work only where people kept the law of Judaism. This meant that the non-Jew who entered Judaism was like a newborn child who had no previous father, mother, or siblings. This new birth was symbolized by baptism. The Rabbi who converted a non-Jewish person saw himself as one who had created the new convert out of nothing, or as though he had begotten him. John the Baptist tried to break through this self-righteous stance by calling on Jewish people to be baptized, too. The writer of the gospel of John, with fine irony, took this even further. He moved from the fatherhood of the rabbi to the Fatherhood of God, when he recalled Jesus saying to

Rabbi Nicodemus, *"Very truly, I tell you, no one can see the kingdom of God without being born from above" (Jn 3:3)*. It becomes clearer then why the Gospel writer stressed that this birth was not of human origin. It could not be something a person could will to do as the proselytes did. Rather, this birth would be of God.

Perhaps that is enough to set the stage for understanding this passage in 1 John 5:1-6. The circular question being answered is this: How can one know if one is begotten of God? From our human perspective, only women give birth. For they alone carry the child and experience the pain of labor. But this passage seems to begin with God giving birth. The first verse, more directly translated, reads like this:

> *Everyone believing that Jesus is the Christ of God has been begotten, and everyone loving the one begetting loves the one having been begotten of him.*

The word used to indicate "begetting" in the original language actually means both the "begetting" of the father, and the "bearing" of the mother.

For a moment, imagine yourself a little child, standing alongside a revolving merry-go-round, awestruck to see children riding on it. Someone tells you that you just need to choose the right horse and get on. But which one? And how? They're going so fast; surely getting on is an impossible task. How on earth did the others get on?

Our first response to this passage in 1 John may be a little like that. It's all so circular. How on earth does one get on? How on earth can one determine if one is begotten or not? Each sentence seems to give an answer followed by another that seems to take it away. We are all off-spring of an era which assumed we had only two choices, to believe, or not to believe: either God was, or God was not. We were like the child at the merry-go-round, trying to decide whether we dared to risk leaving this solid, secular earth, and wondering how to go about it.

But the world is changing. The earth is not so solid anymore, and spirituality is again in vogue. Having believed there were only two choices, we find ourselves ill-equipped for the discovery of many merry-go-rounds, all clamoring for our attention.

The Johannine writer offers us a third view: We are already on a merry-go-round, he says. We are already "begotten" of some father. What we need is discernment to discover whether it is the right one. And if it is not, we will need to find a way of being transferred — reborn — to the right merry-go-round. Since these merry-go-rounds cross each other at certain points, knowing if we are on the right one won't be as easy as it sounds. We'll need to look at all the horses. With this image in our minds, let us enter the circular argument of this passage:

In Verse 1: *Everyone who believes that Jesus is the Christ has been born of God,* or *is begotten of God.* Jesus — the human Jesus, with an ordinary human name, whose feet got dusty, and whose throat got thirsty, who wept beside his friend's grave, in anger and anguish at the ravages of death— this Jesus is the one God anointed. This Jesus is the sent one, the promised one. Can't you almost hear the sigh of relief from those who agree with this statement? After all, most of those who don't agree have already split from the Johannine community.

But wait. What comes next in this circle? *Everyone who loves the parent loves the child.* So here's the test of belief. Believing that the human

Jesus is truly the sent one does make us God's child, but we must test the reality of that belief by seeing if we really love the other children of God. The spirit of dissension can so easily grasp those struggling for purity of doctrine. A glance at chapter four will remind us that the writer has been showing this Community of the Beloved Disciple that God is love. Those who are begotten of God, then, will automatically respond to each other in love.

But there are a lot of communities around whose members respond to each other with some kind of love. They could even have some kind of faith. How can we determine if this is the right kind of love and so the right kind of faith? How do we know if we love the children of God? John's answer is strange:

> *By this we know that we love the children of God, when we love God and obey his commandments. (v. 2)*

What we see here is another effort to complete the circle. If we love the child because we love the parent, we must also love the parent because we love the child. Each proves the other.

The word "commandments", at the end of verse 2, seems to introduce a tangent, doesn't it? But not for long. The author moves quickly to include it in the circle by reminding the community that: *his commandments are not burdensome*. By saying this, two parallel images from the Gospel of John are evoked: First, the commandments are not burdensome, meaning not overly heavy or demanding, because they are all wrapped up in the one commandment — loving God with all your heart and your neighbor as yourself. And since those begotten of God naturally express the nature of God, they will naturally want to keep God's commandments.

Some of those who had left the community, by the way, had taken this to mean that the true disciple can no longer sin. This extreme view has been dealt with carefully in the first chapters of this epistle. We can still sin, but it is not natural for us to continue in sin if we are the begotten of God; through confession we will come to the light for cleansing. This is possible for us, because our advocate, the human Jesus, understands our humanity.

The second image probably evoked by the writer's reference to "the commandments which are not burdensome" comes from the farewell words of Jesus, as recorded in the Gospel of John (15: 4a, 5, 7, 10, 12) in which abiding in Him is linked with keeping the commandment to love one another. Because this passage is so familiar to this community, they are not surprised to meet the word "faith" again in verse 4. (The word "faith" here, by the way, is the same word translated "believes" in verse 1.)

> *For whatever is born of God conquers the world. And this is the victory that conquers the world, our faith.*

Faith is the abiding which links the begotten to the Begetter, and which also keeps them there. The world order, or cosmos which is overcome here by love and trust (or faith) is the world order governed by hate and mistrust. And, to bring everything full circle, all this depends on recognizing that the human Jesus is the Son of God — the one who came by water and by blood. Jesus came not with the water only, but with the water and the blood.

Four important words come together in verse 6. These four words indicate where we are to rest our faith. The words are "Jesus," "Christ," "water" and "blood." Like the horses on the merry-go-round, they belong together.

In all the Johannine writings, to call Jesus the "Christ" is to speak of the human Jesus as the one sent from God who reveals God and in that revealing or manifestation brings life. The salvation comes because the human Messiah (that is the Christ) turns out to be the Son of God.

The "water" mentioned in verse 6 probably refers to Christ's baptism. It appears as though some of those who had left the church believed that Christ was a heavenly being who temporarily joined his spirit to that of the human Jesus at his baptism, so that he could reveal God's power. However, he left him again before his death, so it was only the human Jesus who died on the cross. This was because in Greek thinking, God could not possibly have anything to do with that which was material or corruptible. So Jesus could not possibly become flesh and blood and then die. But this was precisely what the gospels claimed he had done. And this is what the writer is also insisting on here.

So how does believing that Jesus is the Christ, the son of the living God — that he is both human and divine — prove that we are begotten of God? Well, it doesn't, of course, if we separate believing from being. But if we truly believe in this human/divine Jesus, the promise is that God takes the initiative and begets us. He lifts us off the wrong merry-go-round, so to speak, — or better, plucks us out of the wrong family, and begets us again into his own. If we are begotten of God, we will manifest God's nature. The essence of that nature is the kind of love Jesus Christ demonstrated both in his life and in his death. This love stands over against evil and overcomes it with the only weapon evil cannot duplicate —

the weapon of self-giving love.

God, and those begotten of God, are clearly differentiated from the evil one, to whom, according to 1 John 5:19, the whole corrupt world belongs. This is decisively different from some of the ancient religions being rediscovered by many North Americans, who see God not as a Trinity, but as a Quaternity, containing within himself both the evil and the good, or who see God as so utterly transcendent that he is removed from both good and evil, much as those who left the Johannine community believed.

Some weeks ago, in the middle of preparing for exams, I reluctantly took time off to dash to the drugstore for some mundane items. A surprisingly few minutes later, I was driving home, tears streaming down my face, exams having become mundane and unimportant. The radio was on in the car and I found myself listening to an interview with a mother in Vancouver who had just received several desperate telephone calls from her daughter, a prostitute in Winnipeg. One of the calls had been taped and was being played over the air in an effort to track down where she was. Her name was Francesca. She was being held by someone named Tony. She was clearly heavily drugged, was being abused, feared she would be killed — said they had slashed her fingers, and knew only that she was somewhere on Broadway.

As you hear me tell this, I wonder, who are you identifying with? Whose feelings are you feeling? I felt as if I were that mother, receiving that call in my own kitchen. I had not planned on such an emotional excursion, but there I was, weeping her tears, thinking, "Some things are beyond what anyone can bear!"

And my next question, wrung from me, was this one: "Where are you God? Where are you now, in this moment, in relation to this? Where are you in relation to all the other Francescas and Tonys in the world?"

I found myself remembering some words from Isaiah. For the writer of Isaiah, in the middle of the terrible things Israel was doing and experiencing, discovered in his own grief the grief of God. In doing so, he found himself entering the Mother-heart of God. According to Isaiah 49:14, he heard Zion saying, *"The Lord has forsaken me, my Lord has forgotten me."* And he heard God answering, *"Can a woman forget her nursing child, or show no compassion for the child of her womb? Even these may forget, yet I will not forget you"* (49:15).

According to chapter 66, a chapter filled with birth images, Isaiah heard God promising the exiles, who feared they would never return to Jerusalem, *"this is the one to whom I will look, to the humble and contrite in spirit, who trembles at my word... As a mother comforts her child, so I will comfort you."* (Isaiah 66:2, 13) But the Mother-heart of God is of course also the Father-heart of God. They are the same. For it was Isaiah who spoke these words — because he felt them, and wept. As later Jesus wept at the death of all the brothers of women like Martha and Mary; and at the death of all the Jerusalems, including ours. Surely in his death he has been in travail with our griefs and has carried our sorrows, that we might be begotten of him. It was this God, surely who hung dead on a rough tree, blood and water pouring from a human wound, because he had chosen to overcome the evil one with that one weapon evil could not duplicate.

The answer that came to me as I drove home listening to that mother searching for her daughter, and that daughter crying out to her mother, was the Johannine answer: God is here in my tears. He was there in that mother desperately praying to God and mobilizing all human resources to find her daughter. And God was in that radio announcer using his position to help her.

Through us, God is wherever the flesh and blood Jesus would have been. This means that God is also there in every human effort to rescue and transfer the Tonys and Francescas from the merry-go-round of this hate-engendered Cosmos to the KOSMOS that runs on love — God's love — as expressed in Jesus Christ, the one born of water and blood — not of water only, but of the water and the blood.

The Johannine writer makes it clear that God is the only one whose love is strong enough to lift us from one merry-go-round to the other. God is love. He does not initiate evil. Rather, through the power of love, he overcomes it. Thus, it is utterly out of place for Christians to blame God for the suffering of this world. Jesus has revealed to us the heart of God - the Mother-Father heart of God.

Actually, Israel had already learned this a long time ago through God revealing himself to Moses as the God who cares for the oppressed, for the widow and the orphan, through the words of Micah, *"What does the Lord require of you but to do justice, and to love kindness, and to walk humbly with your God?"* (6:8)

Israel just kept forgetting. As do we. God grant us the grace to remember.

All are witnesses
of Christ's empowering grace

LAURA SCHMIDT

Parable of the Wheat and Weeds

Matthew 13:24-30, 36-43 NRSV

For many of us the teachings of Jesus and the parables in particular are familiar. We have a basic idea of what they mean. But the gift of the parables is that in their retelling there can truly be a rehearing as well. If you're like me you read some of these and the message seems clear. Take this text, for example: the parable of the wheat and the weeds. Most of us understand this text to mean that good and evil coexist in the world and that we're supposed to take courage and hang in there because it all comes out okay in the end. And in essence that is right. But thinking and talking about the parable is like life — a general sense of the end is clear, but what matters is how you get there and what happens to you along the way. And too, at points, it is less significant that one stands in the pulpit and says something new than that the old truths get said again. We are a forgetful people, we get discouraged, our vision gets cloudy, our hearing selective. We need to hear even the predictable known things again because often they are so hard to do or so hard to remember in a way that makes a difference.

This morning hear again, perhaps hear anew, the parable of the wheat and the weeds, words for us on the journey today.

I grew up in a household with a list of Saturday chores. My mother would sit down with me and my sister and the list, letting us alternate in picking which ones we wanted to do. I liked to do inside chores - dusting, vacuuming, cleaning cupboards. My sister preferred the outside chores — helping with weeding, pruning, sweeping up after dad's mowing and edging the lawn. This all worked out pretty well until my sister realized I liked doing the inside chores and she could really bug me by choosing to do those things and making me work outside. So I have memories of highly irritated weeding, weeding that had to be redone every couple of weeks. I wish I had been more diligent in reading my little white Sunday School Bible, because I would have loved to give Jesus' gardening advice here to my mother. "Jesus says let the weeds grow." This was Jesus! My mother would have had no recourse. My mother is a godly woman, but would probably have had to say that from a gardening standpoint Jesus gives very bad advice here. Of course this is not an episode from *Better Homes and Gardens*. This parable isn't really talking about gardening. It's a commentary on life in this world. It's a story about the way the kingdom looks now with a glimpse of how it will look in the end.

We read the parable and perhaps the situation seems a little forced, with someone intentionally sowing weeds in someone else's field. But this sort of thing really did happen. It was common enough and problematic enough to warrant an official Roman law against it. There was a substantial penalty under the law for sowing weeds in another person's field. It was often an act of revenge or part of a feud. Think of it as the first century version of industrial espionage — you attack the economic livelihood. Were Jesus to tell this parable today it might go something like this: "The kingdom of heaven may be compared to someone who owned a factory that made good computer disks. But while everyone was asleep an enemy came and put bad disk parts with viruses among the good disk parts, and then went away. So when the good parts were being made into disks, the bad parts appeared also. The workers came to the owner and said, 'Did you not have good disk parts in this plant? Where have the bad disk parts come from?' He answered, 'An enemy has done this.' The workers said to him, ' Then do you want us to go and gather them? ' But he replied, ' No, for in gathering the bad parts you may damage some of the good parts. Wait until they are assembled for marketing, then I will have our experts trash the bad disks and keep the good." (Thus endeth the reading...)

Computer disks or wheat and weeds, Jesus is talking about good and evil and about who gets to do what in relationship to each. Jesus' hearers would have understood the farmer's problem, and the options available to him. The word for weeds here is *zinzania*. This weed is an annual grass called bearded darnel that grows among wheat and looks a lot like it. In early stages of growth it looks so much like wheat it's nearly impossible to tell the two apart. Once the darnel and wheat have headed out the difference is clear, but by that time the roots have become so intertwined any attempt to pull the weeds will uproot the wheat as well. Darnel doesn't grow as high as wheat, so sometimes the wheat is harvested over top of it and then the weeds are set on fire. But most often the reapers separate wheat and weeds as they cut. It makes for a slow, tedious harvest but little of the wheat is lost this way. Seen in this context of agricultural reality (rather than our own tedious gardening experiences) it is not quite so surprising to hear Jesus say "let it grow," although the choice is for a difficult harvest, a messy field and growing season.

The parable addresses a number of questions. The most obvious of these is the question of evil. Whether it is the figure of Job, hundreds and hundreds of years old, or a 20th century rabbi, we find ourselves asking why bad things happen to good people. The problem of evil concerns all of us. How did evil get here? Why is it still allowed to flourish? How can a loving God allow the destruction, the oppression, the injustice we have seen in the 20th century alone?

The servants in the parable want to know where the weeds came from. The master's answer is simply "an enemy has done this." That's all they get, and it's on to other matters. They probably wanted a better explanation; we want a better explanation, don't we, of why it's this way? Why evil? An explanation would make enduring it more bearable somehow. Or would it? Maybe it's like what Frederick Buechner (*Wishful Thinking: A Seeker's ABC's*. 1993) says about Job. Job wants an explanation for all these terrible things that have happened to him. Job wants his day in court with God. But suppose God had actually explained why all of his sons and daughters were killed? Job would have his explanation, but what then? Job would have still had to face his children's empty chairs at breakfast every morning. Explanation doesn't always change a lot about living out the reality. In Job's case he doesn't get an explanation but gets God himself in the end, and suddenly the need for explanation fades. I'm not saying we shouldn't ask why. But in truth, explanation doesn't always change a lot about living out the reality.

The reality the parable makes clear is that wheat and weeds coexist for now. How are we to understand this image of wheat and weeds, good and evil mixed? Jesus' interpretation (vv. 36-43) makes clear that in the field of the world good seed and bad seed grow together. The children of the kingdom and the children of the evil one coexist. Yet there will come a time when good and evil will be judged and separated. The parable is for the seeds growing in the field, for us. It is for those living in the time between sowing and harvest, the time between the inauguration of the kingdom and the kingdom's coming in its fullness.

The parable functions as assurance to those who look around and see the impact of God's reign as ambiguous, even dubious at times. It took faith for people to believe that the kingdom had come with Christ; it was hard to tell at points. It's the same today. It takes great faith to believe and live the kingdom now. It takes great faith, as we look across the table or across the street or across town or across the world and see that the lame do not walk, the blind do not see, the poor do not have good news, the oppressed are not free. The parable is an assurance that despite the ambiguity of our present experience, the kingdom of God is at work and will ultimately triumph. Jesus' acknowledgment of the coexistence of evil and good is an encouragement when we are tempted to be discouraged by the evil in this world. Surely this part of the parable's message needs to be heard and said, again and again.

Jesus' interpretation identifies the seed as the children of the kingdom. But as we hear the parable itself, we tend to identify with the servants, don't we? I think this is all right. The servants are trying to do their job, they come to their lord for direction, they want to help out and do the right thing. But the servants see the weeds and seem to lose sight of all else. They seem concerned that the weeds, left alone, will choke out the wheat. They act as if the weeds would be found stronger than the wheat. And in response the servants seem to want to act not like the master but like the enemy. They want to attack the weeds as the enemy attacked the wheat. Now, we are to be concerned with the weeds of thought and action that grow against the seed of the kingdom. This is not a "free and easy" parable. Matthew's portrait of Jesus is not that of a free and easy master. This is the gospel which included considerable teaching on personal and corporate discipline (consider the Sermon on the Mount and a favorite in our tradition, Matthew 18). The parable does not tell the servants to be free and easy. It tells them to be trusting. Is their passion to uproot the weeds (which everyone would know would result in uprooting the wheat as well) driven by faith or fear? Is it faith in God's just end or fear that the weeds just might be stronger? Is the passion driven by faith or power? Faith in God's inclusive purposes in the kingdom or the seductive power of drawing and monitoring the lines of who's in and who's out? Faith or a desire for power? Faith or fear?

I don't know what you think of Halloween. It was clear again this past week that some within the church at large are concerned with what they understand to be the significant power of evil in Halloween. Is this concern driven by faith or fear? Do we have faith in God's overwhelming power or do we fear that the weeds just might be stronger? What characterizes the concern?

In response to the servants' concern the master assures them of the final separation of the wheat and weeds. The confidence and certainty of the coming separation should help keep them, should help keep us, from worrying about the fate of the seed. We trust in God's just end, we grow our best in the meantime, trusting that our work is not in vain.

We have said that Jesus' interpretation discusses the presence of good and evil in the field of the world. But might we also take it to mean that in the field of the church good and evil exist together? Was this also a word to the disciples anxious to weed out the rabble from among those following Jesus?

In Matthew's gospel Jesus seems to recognize those in the kingdom as both good and bad. In chapter 22 Jesus tells a parable which compares the kingdom to a wedding banquet a king gives for his son. The invited guests all make excuses not to come. And the king says "The wedding is ready, but those invited were not worthy. Go therefore into the main streets, and invite everyone." And it says the servants went and gathered good and bad to come to the banquet. Good and bad. Wheat and Weeds? Remember for Jesus personal and corporate discipline are important — the Sermon on the Mount, and Matthew 18. But might both these parables also warn of expecting perfection within the community of believers this side of God's judgment? Is part of the reality of the parable the reality of wheat and weeds within the church?

Our parable this morning is about sowing and harvesting and the growing in between. The kingdom revolution of God comes in several stages: a period of planting, a period of growth, and a period of decisive intervention. For the first Christians, the question of how to deal with the weeds grew as Christ's return was delayed. The disciples thought that after the Messiah came, the kingdom would be pure; the people of God would be the immaculate bride. But this was not the case. The early church, like the church now, is composed of imperfect people, growing slowly, even haltingly toward the harvest. Perhaps the disciples see this and become anxious, become the servants wanting to do the task of the reapers. But the master's response makes clear it is not that time yet, it's still the time for growing. The "promiscuity of good and evil" as one scholar calls it, is inevitable for now.

And a close look reveals that even when it is the time for harvest the gathering and separating is not the servant's job. I had never noticed that, had you? The servants are not the reapers. They don't do the gathering and sorting. Jesus' interpretation (vv. 36-43) identifies the good seed as the children of the kingdom. At some level in the telling of the parable we are also the servants I think, ready to help do the work, hoes and spades in hand. (We need to clean this place up!) Whether we are the servants or the seed or both, one thing is clear. We are not the reapers. As seeds, our task is to grow with tall stalks and full heads of grain reaching toward the sky. As servants, we are told to endure, letting both grow until the end. "And at harvest," the master says, "I will tell the reapers to collect the weeds and wheat." Not "wait until harvest and then you can separate out the weeds from wheat." Not "at harvest the grain will rise up and swallow the weeds for the children of the kingdom are mightier than the children of the evil one." No, rather, " at harvest I will tell the reapers and they will collect and separate." The interpretation explains *"The Son of Man will send his angels, and they will collect out of his kingdom all causes of sin and all evildoers. Then the righteous will shine."* A wonderful promise for us. But the weeding decision is never ours to make. Our knowledge of good and evil is never deep enough to purge another from the kingdom. Only God sees that clearly.

What does this mean? At what level or in which direction are we able to discern good and evil? Does this mean we can make no judgment about another's actions? How does accountability factor in? (What about Matthew 18?!) How can we tell when we're crossing over into "reaper" activity? Is it a question of direction? Intention? Lines in the sand? I look forward to our ongoing discussion of this passage after the service — there are so many questions I need help with, so many things left unanswered. This parable, perhaps like many, was clearer from a distance than from up close.

But what is clear? It is clear that we are not the reapers, that judgment of who's in and who's out of the kingdom is not up to us. This should give us pause, I think. What does this mean for how we live with and act toward each other now? How is this a mark of discipleship?

It is clear that in the end good will triumph over evil, no matter what it looks like right now. We can trust in God's just judgment of good and evil in the end.

It is clear that though the current reality is a mixed affair, the kingdom is growing even now. We are called to participate in the kingdom now. We must trust in God's faithfulness and strength.

And it is clear that the challenge for us is living in the time between sowing and harvest, in the time of wheat and weeds, in the world and in the church.

God grant us wisdom, that we may extend mercy to each other as we grow. Amen.

KAREN HEIDEBRECHT THIESSEN

Free: From What? For What?

Romans 8:1-11

Several months ago I watched a film called *The Shawshank Redemption*. You may have seen it too. It is set in a maximum security prison called Shawshank and chronicles the lives and experiences of several prison inmates. The horrors and humiliations of life in this prison are vividly portrayed as well as the longing for freedom that keeps hope alive. When one of the prisoners named Brooks receives news of his upcoming release, the other inmates celebrate with him his anticipated freedom. The day of his release arrives and Brooks walks out of the prison that has held him for most of his adult life and faces the new world of freedom. But the joy of freedom is quickly tempered by the reality of life on "the outside." Alone, without family or friends, Brooks can only find shelter in a poor rooming house in a bad part of town. He searches for employment but finds there are few job opportunities for elderly ex-cons. In his loneliness and in the emptiness of his existence Brooks gradually sinks into a deep depression. In the end, he finally takes his own life. Yes, Brooks had apparently finally found freedom from—freedom from years of bondage, hardship and humiliation in Shawshank but upon his release he discovered his freedom was only an illusion. Rather than being held by prison walls and vigilant guards he was now held prisoner by a life without friendship, a life without opportunity, a life without hope. He had experienced freedom **from** but in the end realized he had not been freed **for** anything.

Although Paul was not in prison when he wrote the letter to the Romans, he seemed to understand the helplessness and defeat that comes with bondage. In chapter 7 he bemoans the inescapable grip of sin that holds him captive despite his best efforts to escape. There he dolefully states,

> I have the desire to do what is good, but I cannot carry it out. For what I do is not the good I want to do; no, the evil I do not want to do- this I keep on doing. What a wretched man I am! Who will rescue me from this body of death? (vv. 17-19, 24)

These sound like the words of someone who has almost reached the end of his rope, someone whose life feels pretty dark and desperate. Paul's words of despair have been echoed in the experiences of many people, maybe even in your life. Sometimes when we have given it our best shot, when we have tried our best to live life the way we know we should but have experienced failure time and time again, we feel about ready to give up the struggle because it's just too hard. Despite our best intentions we repeatedly end up doing the very things we don't want to do. We think that we are finally on the right track and we're making some progress and then something comes along to derail us and we find ourselves lying bruised and defeated in the ditch once more. Often it finally seems easier to just give up trying, to quit fighting the inevitable and to just give in to the forces and circumstances that seem to ultimately control us.

None of this is news for Paul. It is his basic assumption that we are in bondage to sin and desperately need to be freed. He argues that the natural orientation of humanity is not towards God but towards ourselves and towards our world which is dominated by rebellion and sin. He argues that our natural inclination is to honor the created above the Creator, to condemn others and excuse ourselves, to serve ourselves and deny others, to live a life shaped by self-love rather than the love of God. In today's passage Paul refers to this as our sinful nature or in some translations as "life in the flesh." He doesn't paint a pretty picture of this state of being. In later verses he describes it as a way of living that is dominated by hostility to God, enslavement to our natural desires and the final, inevitable manifestation of sin, death. He describes it as a state of bondage and oppression from which we are helpless to escape despite our best efforts. It is a life sentence with no chance of parole.

But the gloom and despair is abruptly displaced by celebration and joy in verse 1 as Paul proclaims, *"Therefore, there is now no condemnation for those who are in Christ Jesus, because*

through Christ Jesus the law of the Spirit of life set me free from the law of sin and death." Jesus has done for us what we were unable to do for ourselves. Jesus comes crashing through our prison walls, throwing off the shackles that bind us, loosing the grip of the forces that hold us hostage. *"For what the law was powerless to do in that it was weakened by the sinful nature, God did by sending his own Son in the likeness of sinful [humanity] to be a sin offering"* (v.3). Jesus became like us identifying with us in our mortality, in our human temptations, and in the weakness that sin uses so effectively to destroy us.

But to say something is like something else also implies that there is a degree of distinctiveness. They are alike but not identical. Jesus, God's Son, became like us in our humanness but unlike us, he did not become enslaved to sin but rather lived a life of obedience to God. This freedom from the bondage of sin qualified the Son of God to become the needed and absolute sacrifice for sin. Sin and death stood by helplessly as Jesus broke through sin's ultimate manifestation which is death and into resurrection life. The resurrection of Jesus signaled a new beginning for humanity. Sin's power was no longer the final word for its power had been more than matched by the power of God's Spirit. Through the faithfulness of Jesus, we have been set free. We celebrate the joy of freedom that is ours because of Jesus' triumph over sin. We walk out through the once impenetrable gate of Shawshank and into the freedom of life beyond the bondage of sin.

But like the recently released Brooks in the film, we find ourselves asking the "what now" question. For what purpose have we been freed? What kind of life awaits us as we cross the threshold from bondage into freedom? Often beauty and home decorating magazines make use of before and after pictures to contrast the dowdy old with the transformed new. Paul uses a similar technique in verses 5-8 to answer the "what now" question as he contrasts the old life in bondage to sin with the new life in the Spirit. While once we were enslaved to ourselves and our own desires we have now been freed for a new relationship with the God who created us. While once we were in a position of opposition toward God we have now been reconciled toward God. While once we were enslaved to death, we have now been given the gift of life. Because we have been set free through the faithfulness of Christ, we celebrate with Paul that there really is now no condemnation for those of us in Christ Jesus. The freedom Christ brings liberates us from bondage to our past with all its mistakes and failures. By the power of Christ's death and resurrection, we are now freed to live our lives on a different level. We are freed to live lives controlled by God's spirit at work within us.

It all sounds pretty upbeat and victorious doesn't it? It is as if we have left all our problems and struggles behind. In some ways, it doesn't seem very real. After all, I know that I certainly do not live a sin-free existence. I am often tempted and sometimes I give in to that temptation. I don't live in some spiritual state separate from the effects of sin so visible in the world around me. It's easy for us to feel defeated and overwhelmed with guilt when our before and after pictures aren't as starkly different from one another as we think they should be.

It reminds me of a friend of mine who experienced a dramatic change in her life when she came to faith in Jesus. I was so impressed with her new spiritual vitality and dedication. She could give a testimony that brought shivers down your spine and tears to your eyes. My own story of faith felt boring and pedestrian in contrast to hers. But several months later when I met her again, some things had changed. She seemed despondent and defeated. When I asked about it, she told me that she was coming to the conclusion that her whole spiritual experience had been nothing more than a temporary illusion. Things hadn't changed for her like they should have. She still struggled with some of the addictive habits that had characterized her life before she came to faith in Christ. She felt like a failure in her faith because she still hadn't been able to forgive and move beyond some of the hurtful experiences of her past. She felt like God had given her a chance to start over again but she had blown it completely.

It's experiences like this that make it important for us to clarify several things that Paul is saying. He is not saying that those who are now in Christ Jesus will no longer sin. He is not saying that we are now exempt from the struggle against sin. Paul is not promoting some sort of impossible Christian perfectionism. What Paul says is that there is no longer condemnation for those in Christ Jesus. For although we will continue to live with the effects of sin, we are no longer under the authority of sin. Paul is speaking more about direction than perfection. To walk or live according to the Spirit of God speaks of an orientation to a goal, a continuous journey toward a goal that has not yet been attained. Paul does not assume that the process of salvation is complete but he does assume that it has begun. He does not assume that our total being has been completely transferred to another realm, but he does assume that a decisive transfer of allegiance has taken place. Paul does not say that moral effort on our part will no longer be necessary, but he does assume that the inner compulsion of God's spirit has become the most important motivating factor for us.

The new life we now share in the Spirit is a foretaste of the life which we will have in full at God's final re-creation of reality. Until that day, we live in a tension between the life in Christ that is already ours and the life in Christ which is to come. We experience the tension and sometimes the frustration of living between the ages as we await our final and complete liberation in the age to come. Paul describes that tension in verses 10 and 11 where he writes, *"But if Christ is in you, your body is dead because of sin, yet your spirit is alive because of righteousness. And if the Spirit of him who raised Jesus from the dead is living in you, he who raised Christ from the dead will also give life to your mortal bodies through his Spirit, who lives in you."* Although we are given life in Christ, we do not escape this body of death nor the death of this body. But something has changed. For God's acceptance, life and power are not subject to sin or death, and when sin plays death as its last card, God's Spirit will trump it. For then even death will be drawn under the power of the Spirit of life and we will fully share in that resurrection life.

In this passage Paul reminds us that we have much to celebrate. We are no longer in bondage, for God in Christ has come crashing through our prison walls, throwing off the shackles that bound us, loosing the grip of the forces that held us hostage. We are able to walk out through the once impenetrable gate of Shawshank and into the freedom of life beyond the bondage of sin. We are also reminded that crossing the threshold from bondage into freedom is not the end but rather marks the beginning of a journey, a journey toward a goal which we have not yet attained in its completeness. This is a journey that will end only on that day when we will experience full and complete liberation — in the freedom of the final re-creation of reality when our total being will be transformed in God's new world.

NANCY RIEDIGER FEHDERAU

Giving Birth to Life in Death

I was enjoying lunch with my parents one balmy October day. The nights were already frosty. My parents were happily looking forward to spending another winter with their good friends in Florida.

The car had been serviced, lists made, arrangements for mail and bills taken care of. They themselves, at 84 and 87, had had their last checkup with the doctor, who confirmed their status of good health and wished them well on their journey. Just before leaving, Mom thought she would mention to him that lately she could not eat as much as she used to, always felt full, and had lost some weight over the last months. The doctor ordered a stomach x-ray, just to make sure. More than a week had passed since that x-ray. She thought it would be good to have the results before they left. I assured her that if we didn't hear anything in the next few days, I would call for the report just to set her mind at ease. We continued to talk of good times and shared family news. She was always interested to hear what her two great grandchildren were up to ... Then the telephone rang.

In the space of a few moments our world was turned upside down: an enormous stomach tumor, three months to live without surgery, up to a year with surgery. After the initial shock, we looked deep into each other's eyes. Mine were swimming with tears. She calmly said, "Don't cry. We will take from the Lord whatever comes. If that's the way it has to be, then so be it." We suddenly found ourselves on a fast train, heading in directions over which we had no control. The tumor could not be removed, so the doctor elected to perform a stomach by-pass.

Mother lived one month longer than the year given her. We cared, we loved, we cried, we shared and talked about life, death and dying. We encouraged each other and we prayed as our family walked with Mom along this part of her journey. It was hard watching her optimistic, courageous, and determined spirit struggle and finally give in to her wasting, dying body.

She spent her last weeks in a spacious, bright room in the palliative care unit of a nearby health facility. A cot was provided so I could spend the nights beside her as well. It was a privilege to be free to spend most of my time with her. We had many precious moments together.

She liked to sit straight upright in bed sometimes, but needed to be held and supported in this position. This was rather awkward to do from the side of the bed, so I crawled up into her bed behind her, so she was sitting between my legs, leaning up against me. As I sat there quietly holding her from behind, my thoughts drifted and a picture unfolded: a farm house during a blustery March blizzard, many years ago. How often she had told me of this event: my mother on a bed in much the same position that I was presently in, giving birth to my life. Now, the roles were reversed. I was in the birthing position, helping my frail, weak mother through her journey of birth through death into a new life - a new life in heaven, and it was taking so long to get there. Each morning, when I would greet her, she would open her eyes, look around, and then shake her head in disappointment. Not yet in heaven.

As I mused, all the while stroking and holding her, I thought of something I had read recently. A mother was encouraging her daughter and told her, "When you were born, you cried lustily, while all the people standing around you laughed. Live well, so that when you die, you will be the one that laughs, while all the people around you cry."

Well, my mother breathed her last breath in my arms one night. She was laughing; I was crying. And then I thought of my own eventual birthing journey through death into life.

GERTRUD GEDDERT

Reaching Out In Faith

Mark 5:24b-34

The text I have chosen for my sermon today is one of the New Testament texts that continually challenges and encourages me. It is also a text that has fascinated me in the context of counseling and pastoral care because it has to do with the question: "How does Jesus relate to people with problems?"

In Mark 5:24b-34 we are introduced to a woman with many problems who comes to Jesus and receives help from him. She had suffered a great deal from a physical problem. For 12 years the woman had had a serious menstrual bleeding problem with perhaps a purely physical cause, but there could also have been psychological causes, for example, resulting from some sort of psychological pressure on this woman. The way her environment dealt with her and her disease definitely did not further any healing; it made it worse. She had not only suffered from her illness, but also through the many things that had been done to her in the futile attempts to heal her. "She had suffered a great deal under the care of many doctors" is what the text says. A woman in this situation, back in the first century, had to do many crazy things and suffer from many humiliating treatments. But "instead of getting better, she grew worse." We can only imagine the shame and humiliation these treatments must have meant for this woman.

The next problem was one of bankruptcy. "She had suffered a great deal under the care of many doctors ... **and had spent all she had.**" She had used up all her money. There was nothing left for her to live on. Most of us have some sort of medical insurance, so it might be hard for us to grasp the significance of the phrase, **"she had spent all she had."** And yet there are people around us, maybe even among us, who understand what it is like to be sick and as a result be reduced to poverty.

Pain, shame, and **poverty**, those were only three of her problems. She had even more! She was unclean - almost as though she were a leper! Let me read the Jewish law that applied to this woman and to the people around her:

If a woman has a discharge of blood for many days ... every bed on which she lies ... everything on which she sits shall be unclean ... Whoever touches these things shall be unclean, and shall wash his clothes, and bathe in water, and be unclean until the evening". (Lev. 15:25-27 NRSV)

This woman was forbidden to have any kind of physical contact with people. She was unclean and she made everyone who came too close to her unclean as well. We do not know if she was married, though probably she had been at first. In the culture of the first century virtually every girl who reached puberty would be married. But if she had had a husband, then in that culture it is pretty certain that after 12 years of being untouchable, the husband would have been long gone.

She was not allowed to touch anyone and no one was allowed to touch her. Can you imagine this? Twelve years without ever being touched by anyone, not even a handshake; in fact, you would be carefully avoided by everyone. Just accidentally touching something she had touched was enough to make others unclean! And that was also forbidden! And so her friends and family had probably forsaken her a long time ago. How could one live a normal life together with a person in her condition?

But there was even more! When she walked down the street and came near people, she was required to shout, "Unclean, Unclean!" and everyone would carefully make a detour around her. She was not only excluded from close contact with people, she was excluded from virtually any meaningful kind of relationship. For 12 years she was totally separated from people. That is a long, long time.

She was also excluded from religious life. Since she was religiously unclean, she was unable to go to the synagogue to pray or participate in the feasts at the temple. She could not bring a sacrifice or a gift to the altar. She must have wondered more than once if God too had forsaken her!

I think the greatest problem this woman faced was probably total hopelessness. How else can you feel when no matter what you try, things get worse? She had spent everything she had; she had endured all sorts of painful and embarrassing treatments. Without a doubt she had often prayed and pleaded with God to heal her, and nothing had changed! She was at the end of her rope!

Then she heard about Jesus and she said to herself, "If I could only touch the hem of his garment, I would be made well!" I doubt very much that this was a huge confident faith; it sounds more like a tiny mustard seed faith. She experienced a tiny drop of courage in an ocean of despair. But she exercised her little faith. What did she have to lose? She wanted to be healed, and so she stretched out her hand and the power of God flowed into her and healed her. In verse 29 it says: *"Immediately her bleeding stopped and she felt in her body that she was freed from her suffering."*

Now the story could have ended right there. She had believed and her faith had led to her healing. But this was not yet the full healing she needed! Only her physical suffering had come to an end. Her loneliness, social unacceptability, and the inner pain of 12 years of humiliation were all still there. This woman needed far more than physical healing. Have you ever wondered why Jesus confronted the woman and made her tell her story publicly? Verse 30 says, *"At once Jesus realized that power had gone out from him. He turned around in the crowd and asked, 'Who touched my clothes?'"* Jesus immediately felt that something more had happened than just the ordinary jostling of the crowd. The touch had been deliberate.

Why did Jesus confront this woman in front of everyone? Did he not know how embarrassing that must have been to have her situation brought out into the open in front of all these people? Why didn't Jesus let this woman sneak back home, as secretly as she had come?

Why? Because physical healing is not enough. Jesus knows that this woman needs a new touch in all areas of her life. He wants her to be whole, completely whole! Jesus does not want to stop at a physical touch that leads to a physical healing. He wants to change a life, completely! And so Jesus confronts this woman in front of the whole crowd. *"The woman, knowing what had happened to her, came and ... trembling with fear, told him the whole truth"* (v.33). Try to imagine the situation. She was trembling with fear. Was she afraid of Jesus? Maybe. With her touch she had made him unclean, too! Maybe he would scold her. Perhaps she had some of these thoughts. But I think she was more afraid, probably even terrified of the crowd. What would they do? She had broken all the rules. Would her deepest fears come true? Would they stone her? Would they all shout "unclean" and withdraw in horror?

Well, what did the crowd do? The text does not tell us exactly but let's imagine what happened. Jesus makes her confess in front of all these people. And she obeys. She must have been afraid that all these people would just hurt, punish and reject her all over again. Now, how do you think the crowd responded?

Did they do what she feared? I don't think so. When Jesus is present, we don't shout "UNCLEAN." We don't point fingers; "look at her, look what she did! How could she?" No, in the powerful presence of Jesus nobody rejected, condemned, or even thought of punishing her. That in itself must have been an incredible healing experience.

It was tremendously important that her healing was brought out into the open. This woman could not sneak away and secretly rejoice in her healing, for the healing had to be just as public as the humiliation had been! It was important that everyone understood the situation. She was no longer unclean. No one had to avoid her any more. If the healing had not been made public, how could she ever have persuaded the crowds that she was suddenly clean? She needed the public testimony of Jesus that she was clean again.

But there is more: Everyone needed to hear Jesus address her as "Daughter," not "you poor woman," but "**DAUGHTER!**" This woman, who had lost all her important relationships is now called "**Daughter**" by Jesus! And there is still more. Jesus offers her not only healing, but wholeness and **shalom** (that wonderful word for the total well-being and peace that only God can give!) **SHALOM** is a word that means **all of life** is touched. In fact, when Jesus says, *"Daughter, your faith has **healed** you"*, he doesn't use a word that means just physical healing, he uses the word that means saved completely. And when he says, "Go in peace," he's talking about **shalom**, a well-being that touches all of life.

Hear once more how the story ends: "Then Jesus said to her: '**DAUGHTER**, your faith has healed you! Go in **peace** and be freed from your suffering'."

I think this must surely mean that she was healed in all the corners of her life, not only physically, but in the deepest recesses of her soul!

Does that mean that all scars and memories of the pain would be erased forever? Maybe - maybe not. I think that Jesus' words, "Go in peace" signal that a new beginning had been given to her: physically, mentally, socially, and spiritually.

It was the beginning of a journey, a start, a road that would lead her out of hopelessness, into fellowship, back to relationships with God and with people. We do not know anything about how her life continued. But we do know that she left with the blessing of God's salvation and peace for the road that lay ahead!

So how does this text speak to us? We are also in need of God's healing touch. Jesus also wants us to be made whole. He wants us to be people whose lives are surrounded with God's peace. I want to suggest five points that emerge from this woman's story that can also speak to us.

First, this woman gave up on human methods. For 12 years she had done everything humanly possible; it had not done any good. Of course there are human methods that we want to affirm. We are thankful for doctors and for the possibility of getting help through counseling, pastoral care, and therapy. But human methods do not **always** help. Sometimes healing comes only when spiritual battles are won, and no one but Jesus can win them. And so this story challenges us to reach out to Jesus - way beyond what we think is humanly possible, for Jesus has the power to change our situation, to heal our diseases, to make us whole.

Secondly, "she heard about Jesus." That is what we read in verse 27. But surely this woman had heard about Jesus before; he was a well-known preacher; he was a famous miracle worker. But that day she **really heard** - heard in a way that "clicked"! "Maybe he can heal **me, too!**" We don't know how it happened. Just before this story is the story of a man from whom Jesus had cast out a legion of demons. At the end of that story it says the man went around and spread the good news everywhere. Maybe she heard this man say, "Jesus made me well!"

Two weeks ago some of us women were at a women's retreat, where several women shared

what the Lord had done for them. And others could hear, really hear, maybe for the first time. This text challenges us to tell others what the Lord has done for us, so that they can also hear of Jesus.

Thirdly, she came up from behind and touched his garment. In her situation that involved a very great risk, but she really wanted things to be different. She really wanted to be healed. Maybe we need to ask ourselves sometimes: "Do we really want things to be different? Do we really want to be well? What price are we willing to pay to make it possible?"

Perhaps we respond: "Of course, I want things to be different. Of course, I want to be healed." But do we really? Perhaps it isn't all that certain. It's possible that we get used to even difficult situations, and sometimes we fear change, just as much as we hope change will make things better.

The woman in this story wanted to be healed so badly:

- that she was ready to sneak up to Jesus and touch his garment.
- that she was willing to take the risk of being misunderstood, ostracized and outcast all over again.
- that she even risked being scolded by Jesus, for touching Jesus would make him unclean, as well.

This woman wanted to be healed at any price! How badly do we want to be healed? Do we want it badly enough to take that kind of risk?

That doesn't mean we can't go into our prayer closet, shut the door, pray to God and expect him to heal us. Sometimes that's what we do; and sometimes God heals that way. But sometimes the right way is to do what this woman did. Sometimes God offers healing to those who are willing to go to the crowd of people who are gathered around Jesus.

Sometimes God extends his healing to us only when we are ready to bring our secret wounds and burdens not only to him, but also to our brothers and sisters.

I think we are often a lot like this woman. We only dare to reach out to Jesus secretly. Nobody knows that we are praying for healing in a certain area of our life. I am sure there are a lot of secret prayers prayed among us. And why do we do this? Because we are so afraid! What if we were found out? What would people say? What? You? You have this problem? I would have never guessed that! We, too, like this woman are often so afraid that people might point fingers at us and shout: "**Unclean, Unclean!**" And sometimes there is reason to be afraid. People do point fingers; Christians too. They condemn and ostracize where they ought to love and forgive.

But this is where the powerful message of this text comes in: When Jesus is present, when we are gathered together and Jesus is among us, then we do not do what we might naturally do; we accept and love; we don't reject and condemn. And to experience this is to experience healing and shalom.

Fourthly, the woman stretched out her hand and touched Jesus. Actually she touched only his garment. But she reached out. She could have stood there contemplating the situation forever. If she had not in the end stretched out her hand, she would not have been healed.

God's healing doesn't come in response to thinking about it. She had to take the risk of faith. But she didn't have to have some big faith - just enough to reach out.

When we come to Jesus with our wounds and injuries, we don't have to try to work up a mountain of faith. It doesn't depend on having exactly the right prayer formula, exactly the right words at the right time. God's healing touch comes when we reach out from a longing heart. He may not always perform an instantaneous healing, but let's not exclude that possibility either! Are we ready to reach out?

Lastly, she fell before him and told him the whole truth. When Jesus confronted the woman, she told him the whole truth, not only the facts of her physical problem. When she realized that she could not secretly sneak away, she opened up to him completely, and so she could also be completely healed. As long as we are unwilling to face the whole truth about our problems, how can we expect to be completely healed by Jesus?

It is my prayer this morning that our church — especially our home fellowship groups — will be places where Jesus is so powerfully present that we can dare to take the kind of risks this woman did, that we can reach out to Jesus - that even the secret needs of our hearts can be brought to him openly rather than secretly.

Reach out in faith and hear Jesus' words: "Daughter ... Son, your faith has healed you. **Go in peace** and be freed from your suffering ."

FAITH WIEBE

Living Deeply

John 12:1-8

Last week I was reading a *Far Side* cartoon by Gary Larson. A tall, green, parental-looking insect perched on a large, green leaf was giving his young-expectant brood a last minute lecture. He looked into their eager faces and said, "Of course, long before you mature, most of you will be eaten." In other words, "live deeply while you can!"

Our theme today is "journeying together to Easter." We are all pilgrims walking alongside each other, pressing on in hope with another Easter on our horizon. What does the story of Jesus' death and resurrection have to do with our stories? What relevance does the story of Jesus having a dinner with Mary, Martha and Lazarus have for us today? Why would they be devoted to someone who was going to die? Why would Jesus be pressing on in hope on a journey which leads to his own death?

In the story of Oscar Romero, we learn of a shy, conservative man, who after three months of being primate of El Salvador, became a prophet out of obedience to God's call. He saw the suffering of the Salvadoran people and became unusually brave. In those three months, every ear was pressed against a radio to hear Romero preach. His views, however, put him at odds with the rich and with many bishops and priests, including Pope John Paul III. When Romero asked the army to refuse commands and to stop oppressing their own people, he had to reckon with the threat of his own assassination. On March 24, 1980, Romero was shot while delivering a sermon. Eighty thousand people attended his funeral. A massacre occurred that day resulting in the death of 39 people. The Catholic Church was split in their view of this man, but people in the villages and mountains felt that their shepherd was a saint.

Romero is an example of living life deeply. Why were these people so devoted to a person who was going to die? What is it like to be with someone who is going to die? How does this modern story connect with John 12:1-8? How did Jesus live deeply?

Let's look at Jesus' itinerary sheet in that last week of his life. Jesus' last stop was at Bethany where he had raised a dead man back to life. Chapter 11:45 says " *...many of the Jews who had come to visit Mary, and had seen what Jesus did, put their faith in him."* But others did not. They went to the Pharisees. A meeting of the Sanhedrin was called and a plot was soon put into place to have Jesus arrested and killed.

Jesus' next stop was Ephraim, "near the desert." He no longer moved about publicly, but quietly withdrew with his disciples to a retreat center.

Meanwhile, some 100,000 people participated in the pilgrimage feast in Jerusalem in preparation for the Passover. The notion of the Passover casts a shadow on our text. Excitement and tension were running thick in the air. People were whispering, "What do you think? Isn't Jesus coming to the Passover? They were straining their necks, looking around for him. They knew that if they saw him, they would have to report it to the authorities.

Then six days before the Passover, Jesus intentionally travels back to Bethany! John gives us a broad hint as to where the Passover lamb will come from. God himself would provide a lamb for the sacrifice. Such was the forecast of an unconscious prophecy given by Caiaphas, the high priest.

It is within this context that Jesus accepts an invitation to a dinner to be given in his honor about six days before the Passover. He and his disciples are invited. What is the significance of this meal?

Mary, Martha, and Lazarus display risk-taking, tenacity, and vision in inviting Jesus to dinner. They see and realize that Jesus needs support to face the last steps of his journey. The disciples are preoccupied with their own anxieties and struggles. Jesus' friends in Bethany are also living deeply in their devotion to him.

During the evening of the dinner, Martha is busily serving the food while Jesus and his disciples are reclining around the table, talking to each other. Lazarus is also there - a living symbol of hope in spite of John's emphasis on the Passover and the foreboding hint of Jesus as the Passover lamb.

Unobtrusively, Mary walks quietly to a side room and returns with something wrapped in the sleeve of her robe. She taps Jesus on the shoulder and whispers something to him. He turns around to face her. She wants to wash his feet. Mary tries to control herself, but she is so overwhelmed with grief she cannot hold back the tears. They fall unchecked upon Jesus' feet. In her haste to bring out her jar, she had forgotten to bring a towel. She impulsively loosens her hair and dries Jesus' feet. Then, from out of nowhere it seems, she breaks open a "pint of pure nard, an expensive perfume." A flood of tears flows down her cheeks as she pours the fragrant perfume liberally all over Jesus' feet. The sweet smell penetrates the entire dining room and eventually fills the whole house.

What is happening? Everyone turns around to see. Judas quickly says, "Why did you do such a thing, Mary? You could have sold this perfume for a profit!" He scandalizes her act.

But Jesus rebukes Judas and says, *"Leave her alone! It was meant that she should save this perfume for the day of my burial. You will always have the poor with you, but you will not always have me"* (v.7). Judas becomes silent and looks away.

Mary anointed Jesus' feet with expensive perfume meant to be used for burial purposes. One does not anoint the feet of a living person, but one might anoint the feet of a corpse, as a ritual of preparing the whole body for burial. In this act, Mary's tear-filled eyes and heart meet Jesus in a new way. Mary knows and understands that Jesus will die and be buried. At a deep and profound level, Jesus is loved and cared for and he is energized to press on toward the cross.

By her act Mary steps into the life of Jesus to share in his glory and suffering. She represents our participation in the new thing that God does in Christ. We learn how our worship brings us into community with the suffering Lord. Thus, both Mary and Jesus show us how to live deeply!

Jesus' journey into death and Mary's act of love are examples of living deeply. They open up the possibility for us to also live with Easter on **our** horizon. Like the Apostle Paul, we, too, can *"forget what lies behind .... pressing on in hope to know Christ and the power of his resurrection and the fellowship his sufferings ... becoming like him in his death"* (Phil.3:10-13).

Identifying with Jesus and his journey to death, burial, and resurrection is one way to live deeply and be devoted to him in our path to life. Are we willing to live deeply and go the distance?

LORI MATTIES

A Lenten Journey

For the Sundays during Lent I want to share with you some brief visual images that have given me a clearer understanding of who this Jesus is that we choose to follow. As I traveled around Israel in 1992, I began to see Jesus as a very real person who had very real struggles, and who offered a hope that both shocked people and brought new freedom in a world dark with evil.

From a room in the Tiberius YMCA, we hear all night long the slap-slapping of fishermen scaring the fish into their nets. When we get up in the morning they are hauling the nets in, tired from a long night's work, resting in the bottom of the boats among the fish, telling jokes and smoking.

It was people like these, marginalized in their own society, whom Jesus chose to be closest to him. What made you choose these ones, Jesus? What special gift did they have that drew you to them? Was it the patience they had learned in their long nights in their boats? Was it the courage and daring they showed in braving an unpredictable sea? Was it their willingness to leave all they knew and loved to go with you on the journey? What gifts do we bring, Jesus, that you have chosen us?

Jesus lived and ministered among people whose situation was not unlike that of modern Israel. His words and actions shocked and enraged, and comforted and freed, those around him. He deliberately chose a path that led to suffering.

Lord Jesus, as we walk with you on the way to the cross, tell us who we really are. Amid the confusion of many voices, we need to hear you clearly. Like Jacob, who wrestled with you for a blessing, we need to be reminded that we are called by your name. Like the woman at Jacob's well, we are all outsiders, in need of honesty and the compassion that will allow us to be truly ourselves in your presence. Like Peter who refused to be identified, we need to discover that on the journey of the cross we are truly loved.

What are we looking for, Jesus, as we journey with you on the way to the cross? Are we passing through, not looking, when you bring healing and new life? Are we looking for something else when, through suffering you bring new hope to your people? Where is your kingdom, Lord, if not here and now in the community of your people, where we meet and remember you in the everyday acts of breaking bread and drinking wine?

Jesus, we want to learn from you in your choosing to follow a path so seemingly opposite to common human sense. We choose to be loyal to you, to follow you on the way to the cross, to give up our own power for the love of others. Along the way, we pray for healing of the wounds that mar our ability to love and be loved. We pray for the ministering of the Holy Spirit to fit us for the journey, to feed us for the task of discipleship.

Jesus, you were welcomed into the world by your people. And in your journey to the cross you performed the ultimate act of hospitality in laying down your life for your friends. May you so enter our lives as we journey with you that we too might embody the hospitality of your love.

So here we are, at the end of Lent, almost at the end of our journey with Jesus to the cross. We, too, walk with him down the Mount of Olives, and we, who know the end of the story are not sure whether to shout "hosanna" to our king, or weep for what is about to occur. But Jesus accepted the hosannas. He was and is our king, more so than the crowds then could have imagined. And so it is fitting, as we prepare to enter a week where we remember our sin, our propensity to conflict and even violence, to celebrate the coming of our king into the holy city, the city that is a microcosm of our very lives.

Jesus, as we walk down the mount together, praising you and remembering your coming suffering, we proclaim you King and Savior. We offer you hosannas, knowing the cost and accepting the paradox of a kingdom inaugurated by your suffering, death and resurrection.

Lord Jesus, friend and master of the journey, have mercy on us.

ELFRIEDA SCHROEDER

Mary Magdalene

John 20:1-18

I shall never forget my early morning walk to the tomb nor the long night preceding it, the night after Jesus was crucified. I lay awake and many thoughts passed through my mind — pictures of Jesus who had meant more to me in the past three years than any other person on earth.

I can't recall much of my life before I met him, only that it was bitter confusion and chaos, aimless wandering in a black world — demon possessed they called me. But after Jesus came the darkness and the aimlessness left. He made my life bright and I could live again. I lived for him. Wherever he went I followed, trying to anticipate his needs, ministering to him as much as I was able. There was so little I could do for him in comparison to what he had done for me. Every day I watched him give of himself to others until that last and terrible day when he gave himself completely. I watched in Pilate's court as he was mocked and beaten and the crown of thorns was pressed into his brow. Why were the people so blind? If only they had seen him and experienced his love and healing touch as I had, they would know that he was innocent of all they accused him.

Over and over again I relived the agony of following him to the cross only to stand in its shadow and weep as they nailed him to it. Darkness and despair filled my heart as we took him from the cross and brought him to the tomb. Everything was finished. Would I go back again to the darkness that possessed me before I met him?

The next morning as the dawn slowly brightened the sky, I too awakened to the fact that Jesus had healed me completely and I could never go back to what I had been before. With some of the other women I decided to go once more to his grave. He was still so much a part of my life that I needed to do something for him. I took some sweet smelling spices and went out. As I met the other women we talked about Jesus and what he had meant to us. What would we live for now that he was gone?

When we got close to the tomb I suddenly realized that our morning walk was probably in vain. We had forgotten about the huge stone that had been rolled in front of the opening. Who would move it for us? To our surprise when we got there, the stone had been rolled away. No doubt someone had stolen his body. Was it not enough that they killed him? Did they have to take him even after he was dead? I ran to tell Peter and the other disciples. When they looked into the tomb they too saw that it was empty.

I stood by the tomb and wept, overcome by despair. The last service I wanted to do for him was denied. Suddenly I heard someone asking me why I was crying. I saw two men dressed in white. I told them someone had taken Jesus away and I didn't know where to find him. As I turned around, another man stood beside me. He also asked me why I was crying and for whom I was looking. Through my tears, I thought it was the gardener. I begged him to tell me where they had put Jesus. He looked at me and called me by my name. In a flash I knew it was Jesus. I wanted to reach out and touch him just to make sure he was real. But he asked me not to because he had not yet gone to the father. He told me that he would soon be going to his father and my father, and to his God who was also my God. I didn't really understand what he meant, but it was Jesus speaking and he was telling me that we would be together again. I believed him as I always had. I ran to the disciples and told them everything. They didn't believe me, but I knew it was true. Jesus was with me again!

I saw the morning star still flashing in the sky. Jesus is my bright and morning star who will never leave me or forsake me! He has risen from the dead and is with our father and our God. My heart sings for joy!

BARBARA NICKEL

I'm Nobody, Who Are You?

It is a paradox, where I put to death the notion that I have to be Somebody in this world. I am not concerned with the results of my actions in this world, because through God's grace, through Jesus' death and resurrection, I am Somebody in the kingdom.

Through God's grace, we can rewrite the ending of our stories. We may come from a long line of people who needed the results of actions in order to feel worthy. But perhaps as we learn more about God's kingdom, we can let go of the need to produce a resume when we're introduced to someone, can let go of the feeling that we have no right to be here unless we achieve, can let go of the pride and the self-abasement. Then, as a Nobody in this world and a Somebody in God's kingdom, we can turn to the person next to us, ask, "Who are You?" and truly listen to their answer.

CARLEY FRIESEN-BLANK

The Sign of Belonging

Isaiah 43:1-3 • Romans 6:3-4; 8:38-39

It was another hot, dry, windy day in Kansas. Yet another farmer's family was having a sale. Tools, furniture, farm implements, even house and land were on the auction block. Whatever could fit into the car was packed in, along with the children and the ever-present dust. Mother had been baking for a week, making enough zwiebach to fill a trunk. It was the only thing they knew they would have to eat during the long trip across the country and for who knew how long thereafter. Zwiebach would keep them alive. And so, they set out to find a new home, with their faith in God and a trunk full of zwiebach.

This was how my father came to California as a child. It is also the story of my great grandfather's trip from Russia by ship: empty pockets, full hearts and a trunk full of zwiebach. They were simple people who only wanted a place to work hard and to worship God in freedom. Zwiebach was the "staff of life" for them.

Many of my generation no longer bake zwiebach. It takes too much time and we don't need to do it. So now zwiebach have begun to be a specialty item, made for special family gatherings. They are no longer the "staff of life." And the zwiebach have begun to show up displayed under a dome on a curio shelf, or as a paperweight on a cluttered desk. Why? Because the zwiebach is still a symbol of the "staff of life." They tell stories of the faith of our parents and our parents' parents. It is a reminder of what little we really need to get along — faith and a trunk full of zwiebach.

Zwiebach are, for me, a little like sacraments. They remind me of all the good things my parents received from God and when I eat one, I also enjoy what God has done for me.

The classic definition of a sacrament is: "An outward and visible sign of an inward and spiritual grace." Sacraments are acts of worship, which provide special ways for the body of believers to celebrate God's loving presence in our lives.

They speak to our five senses more than to our minds for our senses are a much more powerful memory system than are our brains. Let me show you what I mean. Zwiebach touches four of the five senses — seeing, touching, tasting, smelling (I could not figure out how you might be able to "hear" zwiebach!) By activating the senses, zwiebach accomplish at least four things:

1. They tell a story. Zwiebach reminds me of the story of my parents' hard, simple life of faith.

2. They inspire me. I am motivated by my parents' story of self-sacrifice and commitment. I want to live up to their ideals, what they would want for me. I want to be able to say, "It runs in the family!"

3. Zwiebach make me one with those who have gone before me. We eat the same food, share the same memories, and so we are one family. We are joined to each other by an invisible bond which connects our very souls.

4. Zwiebach does something more than remind, inspire and create community because I can eat it. It physically enters my body and gets converted into energy which I can use for strength to carry out the ideals we share. It not only reminds, but through it I receive the strength it promises.

That is a lot to get from a simple piece of bread, but at least this much is given by each of the sacraments which we celebrate in the church. The sacraments of baptism and communion are the sacramental acts shared by almost all Christian fellowships, though they may be understood a little differently in each. Jesus instructed us to do these two acts. I think he wanted to make sure there are at least a few moments when we would sit still and let God give us the gifts of God.

Now, let us look specifically at baptism. What story does it tell? What does it inspire us to do? With whom does it unite us? What grace of God is given?

We live in an age of crisis in belonging. The statistics are staggering — single-parent homes, divorce rates, homeless people living on the streets, transients moving from job to job. Or perhaps closer to home: How many of us grew up near our grandparents? How many of us have made a hobby of packing and unpacking moving boxes? How many schools did we attend? Unlike the lessons of many of our life experiences, we want stability. We all want to belong somewhere, to someone. We want to be loved and to know it will last. Isaiah 43:1-3a says:

> *But now, this is what the Lord says — he who created you, O Jacob, he who formed you , O Israel: 'Fear not, for I have redeemed you; I have summoned you by name; you are mine. When you pass through the waters, I will be with you; and when you pass through the rivers, they will not sweep over you. When you walk through the fire, you will not be burned; the flames will not set you ablaze. For I am the Lord, your God, the Holy One of Israel, your Savior.*

Perhaps an even better description is found in God's words to Jesus at his baptism, "You are my beloved child."

What story does baptism tell? It tells the story of our conversion. Baptism is the acted story of change — change from one person into another, of dying to one life and being raised to a new life. In Romans 6:3-4, Paul says, *"Don't you know that all of us who were baptized into Christ Jesus were baptized into his death? We were therefore buried with him through baptism into death in order that, just as Christ was raised from the dead... we too may live a new life."* The old self is dead, a new child of God now lives in its body.

Water is a particularly appropriate symbol of conversion and rebirth. It reminds us first of the waters of creation: *"In the beginning God created the heavens and the earth. Now the earth was formless and empty, darkness was over the surface of the deep, and the Spirit of God was hovering over the waters"* (Gen. 1:1-2). Water was that element from which

God, by the creative Spirit, brought to being all that is. It was the original element of life.

As women, we know very well that life is created in water. It is by breaking through the water that babies are born. What better symbol could there be for our new creation, our new birth!

Water reminded the people of Israel of their exodus. As they, by an act of God, passed through the water of the Red Sea, they were taken into the desert to be formed into God's people. The passageway through the walls of water was Israel's entrance into a new life as God's special people.

Water is the element of cleansing. "Wash your hands!" "Did you wash behind your ears?" Daily washing is very much a part of our lives. Jesus sought to fill that washing with special meaning when he told his disciples to go into the world to make disciples and baptize them. Symbolically, as the water washes over the ones there is a sense of newness, freshness and cleanness.

Baptism in water tells the story of change, of new birth, of cleansing, forgiving; of the entrance into the wilderness journey of becoming a child of God — a child God can be proud of.

What does baptism inspire us to do? Since it is a sign of our adoption as children of God, it inspires us to be like our divine parent. Like the zwieback inspires me with the dreams, faith and strength of my ancestors, so baptism inspires Christians to do the works of God — to live up to God's best hopes for us. Each time we celebrate a baptism, we are reminded again of whose we are. We can make our baptismal commitments afresh and receive motivation to do better as God's children in the days to come.

To whom does baptism link us? Baptism is a community event. It is a sign of belonging. First, it is a sign that we belong to God. And second, it is a sign that we are part of the family of God.

Baptism is a sign of our entry into the church. But I do not mean that it is only a rite of initiation into one particular denomination. Baptism is the sign of being joined to Christ — and Christ is one. Our baptism gives us all something in common. Paul is very clear about this in Ephesians 4: our baptism by water and by the Spirit makes us one. Christ is not divided by personalities, denominations, or even doctrines. We who trust in Christ for salvation are all one, whether we agree with each other or not.

Baptism is a symbol of the gift of forgiveness and acceptance which we receive from God. What a wonderful relief! This is why a person is baptized only once. Mistakes cannot undo our adoption. On the basis of Jesus' work and none of our own we are accepted into the household of God with all the accompanying rights and privileges.

I am a fan of murder mysteries. Anyone who has read but a few of these knows the plot where some young person marries an elderly, wealthy person who suddenly and suspiciously dies. Marriage to a young and beautiful person might possibly be forgiven but to include the person in one's will is inviting disaster. But this is exactly what God does. He adopts us and writes us into his will — right up there alongside Jesus! And, yes, God does know exactly what we are like. God can see through us. And, yes, God has suffered, been called the fool, and died for this "rash" action. But it is done. It is finished, as Jesus said on the cross. We are included and now no one can separate us from the love of God: *"Neither death nor life, neither angels nor demons, neither the present nor the future, nor any powers , neither height nor depth, nor anything else in all creation, will be able to separate us from the love of God that is in Christ Jesus our Lord"* (Rom. 8: 38-39). Thanks be to God!

DOROTHY MARTENS

Treasures in Clay Pots

II Corinthians 4:1-15 NRSV

All of us have treasures. Those treasures can be any number of things: a favorite book, a diamond ring, our baby's first shoes, a family portrait. Anything we consider valuable we call our treasures. Mementos from a trip to the Far East or the license plate from our first car are tucked away, hidden some place where no one can destroy them.

After my mother died, my sister and I came across her treasures. There was a diary she had kept when she was a young married woman; a letter from her oldest sister written from India in 1939; a Mother's Day card I had made for her when I was in grade 2. These were things that had special meaning for her. Yes, all of us have treasures.

God has given us a gift, a treasure that is of immeasurable value. In II Corinthians 4:6, Paul calls this treasure "the light of the knowledge of the glory of God." Where do we see the glory of God? We can see the glory of God in the beauty of the mountains, in the power of the pounding ocean waves, in the trusting face of a child. But the best place to see the glory of God, according to Paul, is in the face of our Lord Jesus Christ.

Paul mentions another treasure in verse 4, *"the light of the gospel of the glory of Christ."* What is this light and this gospel? The light is the life, the death and the resurrection of Jesus. The life of Jesus shows the light of God's love for us. We see that God chose to give up his power and status to become weak and vulnerable. He became a baby. What could be more vulnerable than that? He chose to live a life of compassion and love. With that life came persecution and poverty. He became an itinerant preacher in a land of a conquered people. That light of the glory of Christ is God with us.

It is fine to say God is our treasure. But if we are honest with ourselves, we admit we don't feel like we possess a treasure. Treasures are to be kept in secure places like safes, or in ornamental boxes like a pirate's hoard. Some people keep a treasure in a teapot or a sugar bowl. Do you have a safe or a safety deposit box for your treasure? In what kind of box have you placed God? Or do you keep him in a teapot up on the third shelf, safe for a rainy day?

Paul tells us "we have this treasure in clay jars," in pieces of pottery. Not in a safe, not in a box, but in a pot.

When the potter makes pots, there are beautifully ornate, brilliantly colored pots that are made to show and to sell for a big profit. There are other pots made for using around the house. These are everyday pots. They are not painted or glazed, but rather they are frail, easily chipped, breakable. Not only are these pots cracked and chipped; sometimes they don't do what you want them to do. They are not big enough or tall enough or strong enough. But more important than size is the fact that they are usable. It's what pots are made for — being used.

God is the creator, the creator of vessels. We are the vessels. "Cracked pots" you could call us, fragile, fallible and functional. Sounds unpleasant, unattractive, but let's face it, that's us. There are so many times we are sensitive to things people say about us. Our feelings are hurt, cracks show. We become angry and resentful, chips appear. Or we are hurt because we didn't get the recognition we thought we deserved. We lose friends over misunderstandings. We feel broken. Yes, our spirits are frail and fragile.

As I thought of Paul's description of God's people as "clay jars" I thought about different Bible characters, such as the Samaritan woman and Peter, who demonstrated these characteristics.

Look at the Samaritan woman; now there was a pot with a definite crack. She came to get water in the heat of the day rather than at the cooler hours when other women visited the well. She had tried that and had not been welcomed. She had been married five times and was now living with someone who was not her husband. What could be more shameful? The nerve of that woman! And she talked to this unknown man at the well.

When I look at this woman through a counselor's eyes, I see someone who was resistant to what Jesus was trying to do and say to her. She didn't really trust this man. She was not going to

let him get too close. So she didn't stick to one subject but went scurrying off in different directions. She had been hurt too many times to be trusting.

"Are you greater than Jacob?" she asks.

"Give me this water so I don't have to come back to the well and be shunned."

"What style of worship do you think is best, Jesus? Should it be choruses or hymns? Do we lift our hands or do we stand with our eyes closed and try to look pious?"

"Let me state my position. I know when the Messiah is coming. We've even figured out the date!"

Yes, here was a pot that was broken. Like the Samaritan woman, we too can be hurting and frail, not wanting to examine our defenses but carrying with us a family history of problems. Our souls cry for a relationship with God but still become anxious in case God gets too close. Our minds struggle with the knowledge that to be flexible means having to change and that means things cannot stay the same. Yes, we are easily broken.

We are frail.

We are fragile.

Oh, and what about Peter? Now there was a brave man, big and burly, ready to take on the world with his mouth. "Jesus," he says, "Don't talk about dying. I'll be with you. I'll save you. And if that doesn't happen, I'll go with you. You won't be alone, Jesus. I'm here. Don't worry, be happy."

Then Jesus was arrested and Peter followed at a distance. "Don't worry Jesus, I'm right there with you at your side."

Peter huddled at a fire trying to get warm. "No, no woman! I've never heard of him before." "No, no! I've never been a part of that group."

"No, no! I don't know what you are talking about. I've never even heard of him."

Like Peter, we fail at the things we do. As Paul states, we do the things we should not and we do not do the things we should. And we don't succeed at everything. In fact, sometimes we feel like we don't succeed at much. We wonder at God's wisdom in using us. Like Moses, we are only too ready to list our shortcomings. Failure looms high on the list of our characteristics.

But clay pots are made to be useful, and so are we. In order to be functional, we must be fillable. You see, the story doesn't end here.

Let us look again at these two people, the Samaritan woman and Peter. They met Jesus and the light of his glory filled them. The Samaritan woman went back to the city. "Come see this man," she said to the others, "a man who has told me everything I have ever done! He must be the Messiah." And many people came to believe in him as the Savior, the light of the world. What about Peter? "Peter, do you love me?"

"Yes, I love you!"

"Peter, do you love me?"

"Lord, you know that I love you!"

"Peter, do you love me?"

"Oh, Lord, you know everything! You know that I love you!"

"Follow me Peter. Let me fill you, change you. Let me do great and wonderful things through you."

Filled with God himself, we too can become like the Samaritan woman or like Peter. Filled with God we become evangelists and fishers of people, shepherds and leaders in our communities. We are the vessels, fragile, fallible, and fillable. We are the vessels; God is the treasure.

Yes, we are the vessels and God is the treasure. Our inabilities are mixed with God's power to show that *this extraordinary power belongs to God and does not come from us" (v.7b)*. God's strength is made perfect in our weakness. The people I see and the stories they tell make me conscious of the expertise I don't have. They cry to me and I cry to God. "I'm not Freud. I don't know what to do."

"God, I don't have the ability to help."

God says, "Dorothy, sit down and be quiet."

"Thank you so much," she says, "for your help." It wasn't just me, it was God working through me.

What is the treasure? The treasure is the wonder of God's grace, the incredible reality of God's love for us in the face of Jesus Christ. When I focus on myself, on this particular clay jar, I lose sight of this wonderful truth, this light of what God has done for me. When I look at others I see the love of God on the faces of many people. With Christ, a murderer is set free from the chains of Satan to be a loving husband and father, a pillar in the community. A pastor filled with his own self-importance and a desire for more money is now filled with the love of God, filled to be a humble servant to his congregation. A woman overcome with depression and pain is taken in by a congregation that loved and prayed her back to health. Single moms are encouraged with listening ears, child care and food. I see the love of God on the faces of some very ordinary people in this congregation.

A few years ago, when I lived in northern Saskatchewan, I was driving home for Christmas. It was cold. Not the everyday winter cold — but a bone chilling, wind whipping through the fibers of a heavy down-filled parka kind of cold. I stood looking at the flat tire on my car — I was a hundred miles from nowhere and there was no traffic on the road.

"O God." I prayed. "I'll freeze before I'll get this tire changed." But I figured I'd better get started. I was going to get a lot colder before I was through. Then a semi stopped and a man got out and walked towards me.

"Lady, go sit in my truck," he said. "Go sit in my truck and stay warm. I'll change this tire." I saw the face of Jesus in the kindness of that truck driver.

God takes these fragile, fallible pots called people and fills them with a valuable treasure. He doesn't use just the rich and the powerful. No, he takes the poor and the down trodden, the ordinary. He makes them rich beyond all dreams and gives them the power to do more than they ever considered would be theirs to do. In doing so God tells us that we are loved. God is the power that surprises us with the joy of what we can do through him. We can say to others, "Look at what God has done through me. He can do it through you." Yes, because of your example, people can experience the love, the grace and the power of God. The future is filled with limitless possibilities. Fragile and fallible, but immensely fillable, filled with the light of Jesus Christ and with the power of God you can carry to others a treasure that the world badly needs.

Go ahead, show others this treasure. Show others that when everything goes wrong all about you, there is something very definitely right within you!

Be vulnerable, show others you are a clay pot, cracked and chipped. Show others the power of God's glory in the face of Jesus Christ.

SELMA ENNS

The Samaritan Woman

John 4

Forgotten is the water jar as she remembers her fellow villagers. She becomes the bearer of glad tidings. One beggar telling another beggar where there is food.

Can we appreciate the unselfish concern and care she displays by hurrying to tell those in her town? Forgotten are the many hurtful words and the self-righteous behavior of her neighbors. Her acceptance by this man at the well, indeed the Messiah, enables her to reach out to those who have hurt her. She is freed of the bondage of her own lifestyle, freed to become a rightful member of her community, and freed for healthy relationships. This woman's preaching was successful - many believed!

VALERIE REMPEL

In Spite of the Lions

Daniel 6

Our text today is taken from the book of Daniel. Those of you who are Old Testament scholars will recall that Daniel is usually classified as apocalyptic literature. The book contains six chapters of hero stories and six chapters of apocalyptic visions. Our focus today is on the last story which is found in chapter 6. You probably know it as the story of "Daniel and the Lion's Den."

If you were to work out the chronology of the Daniel stories you would find that Daniel is, at the time of this story, a man of some 70 years of age. He has lived nearly all his life in exile, having been taken into captivity as a young man when King Nebuchadnezzar of Babylon captured Jerusalem. Over the years he has gained a reputation as a wise man and has risen in political favor until he is now one of three administrators who manages the kingdom. In fact, in chapter 6 we find that Daniel is so well-thought of that the present king, Darius, plans to promote Daniel and put him in charge of the whole kingdom.

Human nature really hasn't changed much over the centuries. It isn't long until Daniel's fellow administrators and the various government officials under him are plotting his downfall. Unable to find any evidence of corruption or negligence, they finally conclude that the only way to bring Daniel down is if they can find something connected with the law of his God. With this in mind, they go to the king and ask him to issue an irrevocable edict making it illegal to pray to any god or man other than the king for 30 days. King Darius, clearly not adverse to flattery, falls neatly into their trap and proceeds to do just that.

We have the characters, we have the plot — what does any of this have to do with thanksgiving? Let's pick up the narrative at verse 10:

Now when Daniel learned that the decree had been published, he went home to his upstairs room where the windows opened toward Jerusalem. Three times a day he got down on his knees and prayed, giving thanks to his God, just as he had done before.

Now if I were writing this story, this isn't where I would put the "giving thanks" part. I would put it at the end of the story after Daniel's miraculous escape from what looked to be certain death. I would understand giving thanks to God at the point of rescue. In fact, I've frequently thanked God for rescue. But that's not where the author of this story puts it. In fact, after Daniel is hauled out of the lion's pit the focus of the story shifts to King Darius and his response to Daniel's miracle. We learn almost nothing more about Daniel. So, we are left with thanksgiving at a point of crisis.

I have to confess that my first response to crisis is not usually one of thanksgiving. Quite frankly, I'm much more inclined to whine.

"God, why does this always happen to me?"

"God, this isn't fair!"

"God, make it go away!"

Somehow my prayers of thanksgiving are usually tied to the immediate and to my own personal experience.

"Thanks, God, my cold is better."

"Thanks, God, for getting me through that exam."

"Thanks, God ...," well, we all have our lists.

I find it fairly easy to give thanks for the good things I can see and touch. But crisis? That's not so easy. However, in this text I'm confronted with Daniel, down on his knees in front of an open window praying and giving thanks — in spite of the lions. How can he give thanks to God at a time like this?

Daniel doesn't even seem very upset. His unexpected calm reminds me of a man I once worked for who had a habit of responding to the daily crises of the business in a sort of deadpan voice. "Well, isn't that interesting!" and then he'd chuckle, "heh, heh, heh." Somehow we always expected him to explode, to emote — to be as worried about the situation as we were, yet he almost invariably remained calm. I have this mental image of Daniel, reading the decree against prayer and saying, "Well, isn't this interesting!"

Perhaps Daniel simply gave thanks out of

habit. Clearly Daniel had developed a regular practice of giving thanks. Our text makes that point quite clearly: *"Three times a day he got down on his knees and prayed, giving thanks to his God, just as he had done before"* (v.10). He really wasn't doing anything that he hadn't done the day before the edict was issued, or even the day before that. Maybe giving thanks is so ingrained in Daniel that he doesn't even need to think about it, it's simply habit.

But that still begs the question, because even if Daniel has been giving thanks regularly, we have to ask how he has been able to do that in exile. When do you give up looking towards Jerusalem? How do you stay faithful and thankful to God when your dearest hope, the restoration of your people to your land, seems to go unfulfilled? When do you simply give up?

Daniel was in exile most of his life and it seems to me that there is more than one kind of danger in exile. There is the obvious, being foreign in a strange land and culture, at the mercy of those who are in power. But I'd like to suggest that being in exile also brings unexpected temptations; the most significant of which is to identify so closely with the alien community that you forget where you come from and who you belong to. It certainly happened with the Israelites: time after time they found themselves adapting to the pagan cultures around them, intermarrying and adopting other gods.

There are also the unexpected temptations that arise out of success in the alien environment. Again, look at Daniel. He was enormously successful in exile; his reputation and skill were such that in this story he is about to receive the promotion of a lifetime. Surely over the long years of his political career he must have occasionally been tempted to become just a little "less Jewish." And now in the face of this decree, a decree whose sole purpose is his own entrapment, surely he must have been tempted to pray in secret instead of by an open window. After all, it was only for 30 days.

There is always pressure to conform to the standards of the community you live in. And whether Daniel was ever tempted to be "less Jewish" or not, surely we have been tempted to be "less Christian." The fact is that being the people of God in a pagan world isn't easy. Being alien isn't comfortable; and let's face it — most of us like to be comfortable.

Of course, most of us haven't been in exile. But all of us have had the experience of leaving home. And being away from home, even when it is by choice, brings challenges to our faith.

When I first went to college my parents sat me down in the living room one evening and proceeded to give me this little lecture about how I was about to leave home and would be on my own. There wouldn't be anyone there to make sure I got up and went to class or to church, or to monitor my behavior. I could kick over the traces and go wild. I thought they had lost their minds. I was 17 and leaving home to go to a Christian college all of 45 miles away. I had a reputation for being a "good girl" that I'm not sure I could have shaken even if I had tried! I had neither the intention or the nerve to throw over everything I had been taught, and was, as only a teenager can be, a bit offended that they thought I might.

Ironically enough, many years later when I was getting ready to begin my graduate studies at Vanderbilt, a friend took me out to lunch and basically gave me the same speech. I was going to be away from home, away from Mennonites and the community of people who would know whether I was in church or not. I would have enormous freedom to explore, I would be surrounded by people whose politics, lifestyle, and theology might be quite different than mine. My faith might be shaken.

You know what? I understand those concerns better the second time around. I'm far beyond 17 and I know some things about myself and about living away from home. I know that being in a new environment changes the way you look at things. Old certainties aren't quite so certain; there are new questions, new ways of looking at things.

But you know what? If Daniel was ever tempted to be "less Jewish" it isn't reflected in this story. Daniel doesn't forget whom he belongs to; which God he serves. Daniel has been and continues to be faithful to God, in spite of the lions! Daniel doesn't hide in a closet, he continues to pray and give thanks in front of an open window facing towards Jerusalem.

So, we're back to thanksgiving; in exile, in crisis, as a daily habit. What did Daniel have to be thankful about?

I believe that Daniel was able daily to get down on his knees in prayer and thanksgiving because he was certain of God's faithfulness in all circumstances. Daniel believed that all of God's promises to Israel would ultimately be fulfilled. He had infinite confidence in God's power, in God's ability to save. Reread the first six chapters of Daniel. He had repeatedly seen it demonstrated in his own life and in the lives of his friends - remember Shadrach, Meschach and Abednego?

When Daniel looked out that open window he wasn't simply looking back towards Jerusalem in memory of what had been, but toward what he was confident would be. Daniel was looking for the fulfillment of God's redemptive work. You see, earthly kingdoms are temporary; even seemingly irrevocable laws made by human hands are as nothing in the face of Gods' ultimate reign.

Daniel's habit of thanksgiving wasn't based on the immediate, but the eternal. The problem with basing our thanksgiving on the immediate is that we become tempted to view the material things of this life as the primary evidence of God's presence and faithfulness. We become ill-prepared for crisis, and we lose sight of the fact that the battle has ultimately been won. God is already victor.

Recently on "Mennolink" someone shared his experience with cancer. It was an unexpected diagnosis and this person was faced with fairly radical and disfiguring surgery. But what the surgeons found didn't match the pictures and tests they had taken. His life appears to be spared, and his body is more or less intact. In reflecting on the experience this person wrote, " I wouldn't wish this on anyone, but at the same time, it is when your faith gets cornered that you find out how real it is."

I think thanksgiving is a lot like that. The measure of our thankfulness is in how well it is incorporated into all aspects of our lives. I find it easy to be thankful when I'm surrounded by family and friends, when the table groans with more food than I need, or when I'm feeling really blessed. It's a lot harder for me to be thankful when I'm eating macaroni and cheese by myself in front of the television. It's easy to be thankful when our boss thinks we're wonderful, our professor gives us a good grade, our kids behave, there is a check in the mail, or your best friend calls and runs up her long distance phone bill instead of yours. It's not so easy to be thankful when we're slugging it out day by day. When we feel unloved or unnoticed, when we feel far away from home, when we face illness, broken relationships, financial setbacks, when God seems distant and unresponsive — giving thanks then becomes somewhat more difficult.

Not all of us escape the lions. But we are all called to faithfulness in spite of them. We can all give thanks that God's victory is assured. As the people of God we live with hope, confident of the redemptive power of God. Like King Darius at the end of this story, we can acknowledge that God *"is the living God and he endures forever; his kingdom will not be destroyed, his dominion will never end"* (6:26b). Daniel's faithfulness to God is such that he is listed among the faithful in Hebrews 11, the ones who, according to verse 13, were still living by faith when they died. They did not receive the things promised; they only saw them and welcomed them from a distance. And they admitted that they were aliens and strangers on earth.

This is a glorious hope for the people of God. As we celebrate during this thanksgiving season, let us join Daniel in giving thanks to God, for his power, his faithfulness and the ultimate victory that is assured.

All are witnesses
to the Spirit's reconciling power

KATIE FUNK WIEBE

Love Walks Through Doors

Acts 10 • Ephesians 3:14-22

A modern parable

A certain man was traveling with his wife and family in the northern states when their heavily loaded station wagon broke down. The sun was going down. They were a distance from any town. What to do?

As the family waited in the growing dusk, they saw a car barreling down the road. The man flagged the driver and asked for a ride to the nearest town. He was willing to pay him. The driver hesitated. He wasn't going that direction. It was late and he had many things to do as yet that night. Sorry, but he couldn't help them.

As the two men said good-bye, the man with the disabled station wagon happened to mention that his name was Wiebe. At that the other man perked up. He held out his hand and smiled broadly. "Why didn't you tell me you were a Mennonite? I would have helped you at once." He piled the stranded family into his vehicle and drove them to a place where they could get help.

An ancient story (Acts 10)

A Jewish Christian was praying on the rooftop. He saw a vision in which a sheet filled with unclean animals was lowered before him. A voice invited him to eat.

"Surely not, Lord," he replied. "I have never eaten anything impure or unclean." This was not a boast, but a statement—a description of his actions.

The vision with its strange instructions was repeated three times before Peter was interrupted by the message that three men were looking for him. "Get up and go with them," said the Spirit. Peter followed the men to Caesarea, to the house of a Gentile named Cornelius.

Pause with me for a moment at the door to this Gentile home. Outside this door stands the apostle Peter and the messengers. Inside wait Cornelius and his friends and relatives. Peter is a Jew. Cornelius is a Gentile, a God-seeking Gentile.

Peter had been brought up according to Jewish law. He had been taught since infancy to despise the Gentiles. It is difficult to cleanse such deeply rooted prejudice. Peter lived in a divided world. His religious world was divided into two camps with a nearly impassable barrier between. The Jews stood on one side of the barrier and the Gentiles on the other. And there was little crossing over. Now God was saying to Peter, "I want you to go through this door. I want you to cross the barrier."

"Surely not," Peter had said earlier on the rooftop. "I don't help stranded travelers who aren't Jews. I don't visit Gentiles." He wanted to stay in his divided world, which he saw as a God-ordained, comfortable world.

Divided Worlds

Before we go through the door with Peter, ask yourself how you divide your world. As children our world was divided into mostly good and bad. Certain evil places were out of bounds for us. The pool hall was one. We rushed past it, sometimes daring to catch a glimpse of its dark, smoky interior where we heard balls clicking ominously and men laughing. If someone had suddenly required me to enter that door, I would have died of terror on the spot.

The Indian reservation was also on the other side of the door. It was a place to drive through, not a place to relate to.

I also recall how our religious world was divided into General Conference Mennonites and Mennonite Brethren. The GCs were great people to visit with. After all, they were our close relatives. But we never darkened one another's church doors.

When my husband and I moved to Kitchener in 1959, I was confronted for the first time with some strange people called the (Old) Mennonites. Many of the women wore head coverings and cape dresses. The men wore plain suits. How should I fit them into my religious world? Were they Christians?

One day I interviewed a woman from this group for an article. At the end of our conversation, she turned to me warmly and said, "Katie, I am glad to know there are Christians among the Mennonite Brethren also." I was pushed through a door that day.

The way we divide our world depends on circumstances or environment, family background and our experiences; yet not all divisions are God-ordained.

The hungry divide their world into the hungry and well fed.

The politically oppressed into powerless and powerful.

A racist into whites and non-whites.

But, let's bring it closer to home.

When I am sick, I divide my world into the sick and the well, and I long to be part of the well world.

When I am lonely, I divide my world into singles and married, and wish I were married.

When the end of the month comes and my bank account is nearly empty and I still need to pay the mortgage, I divide it into the haves and the have-nots.

When I feel left out of the church world, I tend to divide it into men and women, ordained and lay members, maybe even young and old.

There are many ways we divide our world.

What were Peter's thoughts as he stood before the door of division between Jews and Gentiles that had been in place for centuries? Think of the worst taboo in your world, the type of person you would never allow to enter your home and whose home you would never enter. Think of the person you are very sure you could never have as a friend.

Peter had been taught to avoid the Gentiles, for they were defiled and defiling. They were polluted and polluting.

I recall vividly sitting on a bus in Chicago in the mid-1960s beside a large African-American man — my first close encounter with people of this race. I looked at his dark skin and tried to figure out my feelings. I recall also the student who told me she had learned as a child from her friends that if you touched a black person, you broke out in a rash. But I also remember the African-American Tabor College student from Louisiana who told me that the first month he was in Kansas, he lived with fear. He was sure that at any moment some white student would burst out from behind a door with a knife to keep him from intruding on white territory.

Until Jesus came, the Jews divided their world into "them" and "us." The Jews shunned the Gentiles so as not to be led into their idolatry. They trained them to keep their distance, especially in the temple. A low parapet or fence separated the court of the Gentiles from the court of the Jews. Inscriptions warned Gentiles not to venture into the court of the Jews on pain of death. To enter a Gentile home meant one became unclean.

Peter had the courage to open the door and enter that Gentile home. He could do so because he knew that in Christ there was no longer Jew or Gentile. Through the cross Christ broke down the walls separating Jew and Gentile. His love opened the door for both Peter and Cornelius.

Peter entered without fear because the Spirit had opened his eyes. The glorious theme of the book of Acts is that Jews and Gentiles are made one in the sacrificial love of Christ. In Ephesians 3, Paul prays that the church of Jesus Christ may be "rooted and established in love, and may have power to grasp how wide and long and high and deep is the love of Christ and to know this love that surpasses knowledge" (vv.17,18).

Paul's prayer is a picture of the church without walls when it is filled with the love of God. What kind of love opens doors of division, of prejudice, of misunderstanding?

A risking love

We love God by following him, being willing to take risks and go through doors like Peter.

That means letting go of our prejudices against those on the other side of the door. It means moving out of our comfort zone and letting go of attitudes we have cherished since we were children.

As Christians, we see love as friendliness in the church foyer. These getting-to-know-another encounters are important but are usually fairly easy, involving little risk.

We may also see love as an attitude of the strong toward the weak, the powerful toward the powerless, the haves toward have-nots, marrieds toward singles, whites toward minorities, Christians of this country toward people of other countries who need the Gospel.

We North American Christians have money. We can love. We have social position and education. We can love. We have a rich tradition of spiritual strength and action. We can love.

But we may also see love by comparing our branch of the Mennonite church with other groups of Mennonites. We may feel we are more evangelistic, more concerned about justice, more mission-minded, more open to the needs of others; therefore we love and serve God the most.

People who operate from a position of power say: "Where can we find some poor person, someone less fortunate who will benefit from my love? Where can we find people with problems, so we can hand over the Gospel, money, food, and clothes, whatever?"

Caring: A Better Word for Love

I think we need to use another word instead of love. I like to use the word "care." Christ cared for us. The word "care" comes from the Old High German *Kara*, meaning to lament, to grieve, to experience sorrow, to cry out with.

Someone stuck in a pit is crying for help, so you crawl into the pit and cry out with that person.

When you care, when you love, you step into the other person's shoes like Christ stepped into ours and cry out with them because you hurt with them. During a recent serious illness of my daughter, there were those who came with a gift of flowers or food and left; and those who came again and again and again and waited with us through the darkness.

Christ took on weak human form to understand our pain and sorrow. To be a caring person, you become weak with the weak, and powerless with the powerless. You are willing to become weak with the weak that they might become strong.

Love is welcoming the other person into our lives, not just donating money and food. A recent widower mentioned that he appreciated the meals his Sunday class brought him regularly, but he wished that just once in a while they would stay and eat it with him. Love is seeing the person, not just the need.

Love is discerning the unique gifts of each person, the least distinguished, the least titled. Love means having a liberating spirit, not a confining one. When we love, we draw together. We enter doors without fear even though our instinct is to stay on the other side..

Christ's love shakes us loose from our prejudices, hatreds, and attitudes as it did Peter and Paul and keeps us when we are tempted to return to them.

A listening love.

Listening without judgment is the special gift of those who love. Listen to the story of the man crippled for 38 years —— waiting to be healed. The story says an angel troubled the waters and the first person to step in was healed. The others had someone to help them, but he didn't. Jesus asked him, *"Do you want to get well?"* He responded with some lonely words: *"I have no one. I have no one to help me step into the water when the angel comes"* (Jn. 5:6,7).

As I move about I also find people saying "I have no one. No one hears me." They say these words, sometimes openly— sometimes through anger or rebellion, sometimes simply by withdrawal.

Listen also to Mary sitting at the feet of Jesus, criticized by her sister Martha. Listen to Martha, troubled with much work to do. Which of the diners except Jesus heard either Mary or Martha at that moment? Did someone get up to help Martha with the serving? Did someone support Mary in her decision to anoint Jesus' feet? Instead there was criticism. Except for Jesus, no one saw or heard their needs.

Listening love is not concerned with destroying the other person's argument, with reducing that person to silence in order to come out on top, even when the issue is abortion, homosexuality or the role of women in the church. A listening love means the least official member of the church, even the weakest member, is allowed to speak.

Let's listen to older adults, whose numbers are growing, but who have no visible function in many congregations and who now must find ways to spend time and money to keep life meaningful.

Let's listen to the Gentiles in our midst, the ones without the solid Mennonite name and pedigree. Let's listen also to the Mennonite "Jews" — those we consider the keepers of church law and tradition and whom we condemn as being too slow to change. Let's listen to those Mennonites who are merging in order to break down barriers.

A praying love

People who pray have hopes, dreams and visions for those for whom they pray. Martin Luther King's "I have a dream" speech was actually a prayer of love for his people. We pray for our family members because we have hopes for them. We don't pray for people we are jealous of. We don't pray for people for whom we have no dreams.

What is your hope, your dream, your vision for our church?

Paul prayed that this Ephesian church, besieged by Judaizers, would be a church of love, power and faith. His prayer was his dream. May we have the courage to pray God's hopes for the church. Then we will have courage and power to walk through doors we have kept closed.

DALE TAYLOR

One God, One World

Acts 17:24-28 NRSV

The God who made the world and everything in it ...gives to all mortals life and breath and all things. From one ancestor he made all nations to inhabit the whole earth, and he allotted the times of their existence and the boundaries of the places where they would live, so that they would search for God and perhaps grope for him and find him — though indeed he is not far from each one of us. For 'In him we live and move and have our being.'

Familiar words, are they not? They remind us of one God of all, over all and through all and in all: One God in whom we have our being, one Creator who breathes the breath of life into the world, one Savior who shows us the true way to live, and invites us to follow, one Holy Spirit who makes the dry bones live; one Spirit who is the Spirit of truth and fellowship, of comfort and compassion.

One God, who made the world and everything in it. One God and one world, created in beauty and variety — sun and moon and stars and clouds and hurricanes, tides and times and seasons. One world of forest and prairie, ocean and steppes, lowlands and plateaus, villages and cities. One world of creatures: cats to keep you company, whales to make you feel small, giraffes and elephants to astonish, sharks and grizzly bears and vultures and viruses to remind you that you are mortal flesh. God made all things in the world, and looked and said, "It's good, it's good, it's very good!"

One world that God has given us, with one instruction: "Take care of it."

Take care of the world. Tend and keep it well. And take care of each other. Watch out for the welfare of your sister and brother. Because you are one family. "From one ancestor," Paul says.

The wisdom of this ancient text is profound. Surely Paul was not even aware of all the nations of the earth in his own time, not aware of East Asia or the British Isles or Australia or Mexico, not aware of the people and cultures of those places in his day. Nevertheless he claims God's sovereignty and care and *inspiration* towards all nations. Even the nations have their seasons. None — no culture or tradition, including our own — is everlasting. They change and pass like flowers of the field. And, like the flowers of the field, each nation and culture is valued and precious to God, in its own season.

This wisdom is profound — and, in our time profoundly relevant. Because of the mixed blessing of our worldwide communications networks, we today are aware of all those other nations, their struggles, and aspirations. We hear daily reports from Sarajevo in Bosnia, Grozny in Chechnia and Kobe in Japan. Images from many nations enter our living rooms; we are continually confronted with the range and severity of troubles and enmities that divide the world. What do we do with all this information? Do we have any way of making sense of our world?

I find that this text from Acts 17 can help me to make sense of the world, with all its differences. This morning, I would like to explore with you the timeliness of this and a few other ancient texts for our lives as Christians at the turn of the millennium. Do you remember when "the year 2000" seemed so far away? The movie *2001: A Space Odyssey* was released in 1968. And it was about the future. But now it's here. "The year" is only a few years away.

And the prophecies and projections for that time are coming true, not, of course, prophecies of "the end of the world," not, as I used to hear on the Armstrong broadcasts on the radio, "prophecies of the world tomorrow," but projections of energy crises, of population growth, of food shortage, of poverty. That future is upon us. For our young people that future is their life. What will their world in the third millennium be like? And what will they, as Christians, offer that world?

First of all, they will be a minority. Not because they are Christian. Approximately one third of the world population is at least nominally Christian, about one sixth of the world population, that is, half the so-called Christians are committed Christians. Today's young adults — you, or your children or grandchildren — will be a minority not by religion but in other ways:

by race, by educational status, by standards of health care, by economic indicators. Our young people and the rest of us, as North Americans, are unusually rich, unusually well educated, well-fed, clothed, housed, cared for, insured, unusually safe. And, "if current trends continue," as they usually do, these features of our life, if they continue, will be increasingly unusual.

Both within and between countries, the distance between rich and poor is increasing. And the proportion of rich to poor is decreasing. This is a serious moral problem. For those of us from rich countries, it means that we will be increasingly out of touch with the basic realities of life for most of those with whom we share this one world. For Christians in rich countries, it means we will be increasingly out of touch with the *majority* in the body of Christ. Most Christians, most Mennonites, are found not in richer but in poorer countries. In 1950, the poor in the world outnumbered the rich by two to one. In 2000, it will be four to one; in 2020, when today's 20 year olds are 45, it will be five to one.

World population is increasing, and most of the growth is taking place in poorer countries. So, having said that, I need to say that I don't believe that population increase is the problem. God has appointed the times and seasons of all the nations, and wants to bless them. Despite population increases, there is enough food in the world. Currently, about 35,000 children die each day of hunger-related diseases — but even now there is enough food for all of us. The problem of hunger is not a problem of food production; the problem is distribution, and, underlying that, the problem is consumption. The problem is not that there are "too many people" or that there is "not enough food." The problem is that too few people have too much of everything, and too many people have not enough. Hunger is not a an agricultural problem but a political problem. It is not a spiritual problem but an economic problem.

Already, half the Christians in the world, and more than half the Mennonites, live in poor countries. As the economic gap between rich and poor widens — unless we can reverse that tragic trend — the economic divisions within the Christian community will widen. The church will be predominately not pink-skinned, not rich, not well-educated and well-insured. To be part of the church in the world, we, as pink-skinned, rich, educated, well-fed and well-insured Christians, need to change.

We believe in one God, who has made one world, who is God and Creator of all people, all cultures. We need to live in the confidence of that potential for unity, and we need behaviors, changed behaviors, that contribute to that unity.

Hunger is still predominately an international issue, and not, for us as Canadians, a domestic problem. But there are other concerns we experience here at home, as well as internationally. One such issue is the provision of health care.

The poor-with-us, those here in Canada, remind us that it is dangerous to be poor. We need big billboards with warnings like the ones on cigarette packages: Being poor can seriously harm your health. You may have heard recent reports about the return or resurgence of tuberculosis. Within the population of the federal penitentiary in Kingston, Ontario, as we heard recently on the news, and on the reserves of Northern Manitoba, to take an example closer to home, TB is making a spectacular come-back. Native people in Manitoba are 10 times as likely to contract tuberculosis as those of us with pink skin and European ancestors; since 1992, the

number of cases of TB has doubled among Native people in Manitoba. The world has not been healed of poverty-related diseases — TB, cholera, plague, parasites, goiter, vitamin and iron deficiencies. Unless we can change the patterns of economic development and underdevelopment globally and locally, we will continue to confront the practical consequences of economic injustice.

So how can we prepare our youth and young adults to serve God and God's world in this imminent future? What do our young people need, what do Christians have to offer, in a world of growing injustice?

Our text from Acts 17 gives us the first clue. Christians need to remember that all the world, not just one's privileged corner of it, is God's world: *"one God and Father of all, who is above all and through all and in all"* (Eph. 4:6). There is one God who has made all nations to be a single family. There is one common humanity, seeking after one God. That is the basic reality: "one God" means "one world" to care for, "one people" to belong to.

But in fact our world is tragically divided: by race, by economic status, by education, by access to resources. And these divisions raise a specific challenge for all of us as Christians struggling to grow in Christ and to offer to the generations that follow us a vision of life in Christ.

All of us need three things: **we need to know; we need to care; we need to hope.**

Those of us from rich countries where education, health care, safe drinking water, adequate housing, electric stoves, public transportation, and underground sewage lines are simply taken for granted, need to know that these basic services are not "granted" to everyone. **We need to know** about the rest of the world, and the realities of life for our fellow-citizens and fellow-

Christians in other places. Before we can work for justice, we need to know there is injustice.

Secondly, **we need to care**. In a world of differences, compassion is one of the strongest forces holding us together. All people experience the basics of living in basically the same way: joy and hunger and anger and celebration and pain and betrayal and love are cross-cultural experiences. We can care: and we need to care. Perhaps we who are older can learn that from the younger generations. Several years ago I was in San Francisco with my family. Now, San Francisco is a city with many beggars — many of them veterans of the US-Vietnam War, who are physically disabled or mentally ill. Everywhere we went, we walked by beggars. My nephew, who was seven years old, didn't want to walk by; he wanted to stop, and became very frustrated with us for always passing by on the other side. Finally he burst out: "Can't we just give money to just one beggar?" Sometimes, the young can teach us to care. And sometimes, because they have been exposed to so much violence in the guise of entertainment, sometimes we have to teach them to care. But our model is clear. "God so loves the world." The whole world.

Finally, **we need to have hope**, and to offer a vision that is worthy of hope. Without hope, knowledge and caring are tragic. I have friends who choose not to follow the news. They don't want to know about the rest of the world, because it is too depressing. I know others who are afraid to care too much, because it just breaks your heart. Perhaps more than ever, what the world needs is exactly what Christians can offer: hope. We need to be able to account for the hope that we have, for the fact that in a world of sin, we have hope for the future.

We have reasons to hope. We have hope because we know God knows and cares, God sees the suffering of the world and is working to relieve it. The story of Israel recorded in the Scriptures begins with God's compassion:

> *The Israelites groaned under their slavery, and cried out. Out of the slavery their cry for help rose up to God. God heard their groaning, and God remembered . . . ; God looked upon the Israelites, and God took notice of them. (Ex. 2:23-25)*

We have confidence to hope, because we know God sees and cares and acts. We can offer the world hope in the midst of its suffering because the vision revealed gives us a world to hope for. Let's close with a vision to hope for.

> *I saw the holy city, the new Jerusalem . . . And I heard a loud voice from the throne saying, "See, the home of God is among mortals. He will dwell with them as their God; they will be his peoples. . . ." The city has no need of sun or moon to shine on it, for the glory of God is its light, and its lamp is the Lamb. The nations will walk by its light, and the kings of the earth will bring their glory into it. People will bring into it the glory and the honor of the nations. The river of the water of life . . . flowing . . . through the middle of the street of the city. On either side of the river, is the tree of life with its twelve kinds of fruit, producing its fruit each month; and the leaves of the tree are for the healing of the nations. (Rev. 21:2 -3, 23, 24, 26; 22:1-2)*

The future which is already upon us is an era of cities. By the end of the century, there will be 25 to 30 mega-cities, most of them in what we call "third world" countries. For the most part there will be cities of huge populations, 10 or 20 or 30 million each; cities that do not yet offer healing; cities that offer disease and slums and smog and violence; cities threatened by earthquakes and floods. Yet the Bible's vision of humanity reconciled is a vision of a city.

For me, one of the most marvelous features of this Biblical vision of the city is that it includes all the nations. Our hope lies in our differences, our unique selves and cultures. Imagine: Serbs and Croats; Turks and Armenians; English and French; black and white Americans; black and white South Africans; Russians and Chechens. All the warring peoples reconciled. But, most significantly, the differences are not erased. Listen to this: *"the kings and the people will bring into the city the honor and glory of all the nations"* (Rev. 21:24,26). The honor and glory of the nations, the beauty and variety of each culture are honored, not ignored. The city of John's vision is not a city of uniformity, but a celebration of difference.

And therein, my friends, lies our strength and thus our hope. Not to erase or smooth over differences, but to rejoice in them, so that the marvelous, infinite variety of the created world is reflected in the human world.

But how can we trust this vision? What makes it not just a beautiful dream? We can trust the vision, we can hope in confidence, because of one who has shown us the way of reconciliation. We have confidence to hope because we, together with all the nations, we who had no hope and who were without God in the world, we who are Gentiles have been brought into the covenant of God's people. Listen to this:

Now in Christ Jesus you who once were far off have been brought near by the blood of Christ. For he is our peace; in his flesh he has made both groups into one and has broken down the dividing wall, that is, the hostility between us....... that he might create in himself one new humanity, ... reconcil[ed]..... So then you are no longer strangers and aliens, but you are citizens with the saints and also members of the household of God. (Eph. 2:13-16, 19)

Differences remain. But hostility is erased; hatred melts; fear is cast out. This is what we have, already, in Christ. This is our hope for the world. In a world that is dying of despair and hopelessness, this is what we can offer, for the third millennium and even to the close of the age.

Amen.

RUTH BUXMAN

God's Good Gift of Land

Micah 6:8

I have been asked to reflect with you today on the theology of farming, the theology of work on the land.

The memories of growing up on the farm are idyllic. I experienced farm life as surrounded with goodness; lots of hard work, a father who respected his neighbors and workers, a mother who shared her bread with any and all who came to our door, and a humility and trust that all was well even in difficult times. These are the experiences and memories of childhood.

Now in the role of farm wife and mother, neighbor and boss, I have observed that successful farming has three ingredients. It is dependent on three ways of walking: walking humbly before God, practicing stewardship, and living in community. These three ways correspond to the threefold requirement of our text, *" to act justly and to love mercy and to walk humbly with your God."*

Walking humbly with God underlies all that we are and do. This is not just nodding your head in recognition and then going on your way. It means acknowledging God in all you do.

A farmer who walks out at night to irrigate under the stars can no longer play the game of arrogance. The quiet, the dark, and the star-stud-ded sky envelop and overcome arrogance. She or he is a guest, a recipient, a servant, a tender of this piece of land. In the dark there is no one to impress, there is no one to hide from, there is no one to blame, to curse. There is only that loud silence that surrounds and reminds how little, how dependent, how in need of love and tend-ing he or she is. No longer able to hide weakness, sinfulness, arrogance, defeat, we begin to experi-ence that we are being cleansed and are no longer weighted down by our own arrogance.

Justice, the first injunction in our text, arises out of a relationship. It yields peace, shalom, well-being. Justice includes demands as well as blessings (or in today's language, "responsibili-ties" alongside "rights.") Justice is served when every person, creature, and created thing is in right relationship with every other person, crea-ture, created thing.

In terms of land and farming, doing justice has to do with practicing stewardship. A steward is someone who cares for something that belongs to someone else, as if it were her own. Paul and I are part of a group of farmers who are committed to farming without poisonous substances, keep-ing farm size to a responsible size, and providing tasty, nourishing fruit for people to eat. We put an artfully designed insert in each box of fruit we send out that talks about these commitments.

Biblical justice and Christian stewardship cause us to look beyond our own needs and our own well-being. In fact we do not place ourselves at the center at all, but rather start from the fact that what we have, we have been given as a gift. It is a gift for everyone, given to us to care for and tend, so that it can be passed on for other's nourishment and well-being. When you know that something you are using is going to be passed on for someone else to use, you will keep it in good order.

Having lived a good part of my adult life away from the farm and now returning to it, I have concluded in the two years time I have been back that farming is too hard, it takes too great a toll from those engaged in it to do it for any other reason than stewardship. There are a lot easier ways to make a living than this, which requires body, soul, and spirit. But if seen as ministry of tending and nourishing the earth so that it will be a better piece of land when you leave it, then it is not only worth it, it will bring you joy.

And finally, what does the Lord require of thee? Love mercy. LOVE kindness. Love loyalty. LOYALTY is a quality of relationship that arises out of two people, two entities, being in covenant together. Like stewardship, the rela-tionship has demands as well as blessings. Covenant loyalty is about how we act in community. It is about helping one another, about sharing. It is about discipline. It is about holding each other accountable. Covenant relationships look for a way through rather than a way out.

On the farm we interact within several communities. One of these communities is our neighbors. Neighbor relationships are built up over long periods of time and are passed on from generation to generation. Some neighbors are easy, helpful, enjoyable. Others are difficult and downright obstinate. It takes time, but the second-mile approach almost always turns an obstinate neighbor into a good neighbor.

Relationships are not always easy, because they require that we stay in touch, that we provide direction as well as praise. One doesn't cheat or take advantage of your workers and they respect and give good work to you in return. A respected worker is a happy worker, and a happy worker is a satisfied child-of-God. Micah 6:8 is an injunction to farmers.

He has showed you, O man, what is good. And what does the LORD require of you? To act justly and to love mercy and to walk humbly with your God.

JAN SCHMIDT

Power in Relationships

Psalm 51 NRSV

David, what a name! The name comes from the biblical character we have just heard about in the text that was read. The person is no ordinary man. There are 58 New Testament references to him including the title given to Jesus, "Son of David." There is only one David in scripture, which typifies his unique place. He is known to be an ancestor, forerunner, and foreshadower of Jesus. His life journey took him from a shepherd boy to be the second king of Israel. God's presence in David's life is evidenced in the many recorded stories about his life from the slaying of Goliath, to the return of the Ark of the Covenant to Jerusalem. Since then many boys have been called David in hopes that they too would bring honor to their families.

David was no ordinary man - or, was he? In II Samuel 11 & 12 we see another side of David; it is not the glorious, obedient hero that we read about before and after this account. David had been king for over 10 years. It was a period of outward prosperity and apparent religious fervor. A palace had been built, highways opened, trade restored. Material wealth in the kingdom was secure. Even the ark of the covenant had been returned and placed in a special tabernacle pre-pared for it in Jerusalem. As was the custom, David had inherited the wives of the previous ruler, Saul. In addition, the laws allowed him the freedom to marry other available women and add them to his harem. There were many reasons to be thankful to Yahweh.

Spring had arrived, and it was the time of year to subdue the enemies. David decided to stay at his palace instead of accompanying his soldiers on another crusade. Following an afternoon sleep he decided to get fresh air. As he wandered on his roof top he looked at the surrounding area and his gaze rested upon a woman in the distance who was cleansing herself after her monthly period. He noticed that she was beautiful and sent someone to inquire about her. To his surprise, he knew the woman's father, Eliam, and also her husband, Uriah the Hittite. (Both are named later in II Samuel 23 as two of David's most notable soldiers.) This information did not deter David. He had decided what he wanted and he had the power to get it.

In spite of the wealth of women at his disposal and the fact that he knew Bathsheba's husband and family, David sent messengers to get her, "laid with her" and sent her home after he satisfied his desires. A while later David received the unexpected news from Bathsheba that she was pregnant. David was in a difficult situation. Bathsheba had not slept with her husband for some time as he was in battle and neighbors had likely noticed the messenger activity between the palace and Bathsheba's home. He could be discovered. Taking another man's wife was adultery - a violation of the Ten Commandments. David had to act quickly. He sent word to the battle field for Uriah to report to the palace.

What follows is an attempted cover up. When Uriah arrived, David asked for a battle report. Uriah's unrecorded response is likely indicative of David's lack of interest. After a brief conversation David gave Uriah a gift and sent him home to "wash his feet", hoping Uriah would become reacquainted with his beautiful wife. Unexpectedly Uriah did not go home but slept with David's servants instead. David's servants reported Uriah's activities to David and again David sent for Uriah to inquire why he had not gone home. Uriah responded, *"The ark and Israel and Judah remain in booths; and my lord Joab and the servants of my lord are camping in the open field; shall I then go to my house, to eat and to drink, and to lie with my wife? As you live, and as your soul lives, I will not do such a thing"* (II Sam. 11:11). David was undaunted by Uriah's faithfulness and conspired to weaken Uriah's resolve. The next evening David succeeded in getting Uriah drunk. Even in this weakened state, Uriah chose to sleep with the King's servants. David's plans were foiled!

David was determined to hide his wrongdoing and developed yet another plan. This time David sent a note to Joab, the military leader, to place Uriah in the heat of the battle. Shortly after delivering his own death message, Uriah was killed in battle. David's indiscretion was concealed.

Bathsheba lamented for her husband and when the appropriate mourning was over David sent for her, married her and she bore him a son. An unrepentant David enjoyed his latest addition to his harem and remained undiscovered, or at least unproven. To some his actions of caring for the wife of one of his esteemed warriors may even have seemed honorable.

Although there was no proof of David's wrongdoing, he had forgotten that God had seen what had transpired and noted his actions. God sent Nathan to David. Since David was king, he was also considered the Chief Judge of Israel. The story that Nathan shared with David was not uncommon. A rich man who had many flocks and herds took a poor man's only lamb to prepare a feast for a traveler who had come to visit him. David was concerned about justice and the poor and his reaction was swift and forceful. He informed Nathan that the rich man deserved death and the poor man should be given four lambs. Nathan quickly responded *"David, you are the man"* (II Sam. 12:7).

As I have reflected on this story, I have been perplexed by a number of questions.

1. Why, with all the women at his disposal, would David bother with Bathsheba ?

2. Why did David go to such lengths to cover up his sin and break yet another commandment by having Uriah killed?

3. Why did David not see his own reflection in Nathan's story?

Why would David bother with Bathsheba? What could she offer that David didn't already have? This story can be understood in a number of ways - a story of one man's lust or a story of the abuse of power. I believe it is the latter and it is a story with which we can all identify. We have all been David and we have all been

Bathsheba.

David had ultimate power as King of Israel. His wish was others' command. He could have any person brought to him - as he did with Bathsheba. But why bother? He had many other women at his disposal. Why risk a one night stand with the wife of your trusted warrior? I think the answer is simple. David saw someone he wanted and had the power to get her, so he did. He chose not to restrain his wants and not to think of the implications of exercising them.

Last week's sermon encouraged healthy family relationships. How do we use the power we each have in our families to responsibly create good family relationships? Relationships have the potential to bring us great joy and conversely great pain. Entering into relationship means we can experience new heights of joy — it also makes us vulnerable. Someone now has greater access and ability to hurt us. We all are involved in relationships, be they family, church, work or friends. In each and every one of those relationships WE EACH have some measure of power or ability to influence others.

Power is exhibited in a variety of forms. Power is seen in position: pastor-parishioner, parent-child, owner-employee, etc. Position power is evidenced when one person makes a decision that others are expected to follow. Power is also seen in physical strength: the strongest and biggest are at an advantage here. Power is displayed in communication: the ability to speak clearly, the ability to withhold ideas and even conversation, the ability to demean others through sarcasm and innuendoes, the ability to make a point in degrading ways. Statements like "Just do it your way!" and "Why would you do a dumb thing like that?" are statements that exercise power and influence over others. Power is

not always easy to recognize. In most relationships both parties have different forms of power and use them in a variety of ways.

Abuse of power is when I use my power to get what I want and in doing so injure another person. We have no reason to believe David intended to hurt Bathsheba that day. Bathsheba's needs were the furthest thing from his mind. He was blinded by his wants and just happened to be in a position where he could get what he wanted. David also had the position power to cover his sin by having Uriah killed.

Just like David we all are occasionally so fixated on what we want that we do not stop to see the bigger picture. We are so determined to have it our way, that we do not hesitate to consider how our behavior will affect the other person(s). We have the power to do what we want and we simply go ahead and do it. This is how our story relates to David's. We all have power and at times have been and will continue to be tempted to use it for our own personal advantage at the expense of others. We all have our own stories.

Why did David go to such lengths to cover up his sin and break yet a second commandment by having Uriah killed? David had chosen a path the day he had Bathsheba brought to his chambers. He had plenty of time to reevaluate his actions before he sent for Bathsheba. The resulting pregnancy was only a complication to be addressed, not a time for reflection. Uriah's non-compliance was an unfortunate difficulty. All these problems could easily be addressed by a king. David was not ready to acknowledge wrongdoing after all the trouble he had gone to. Once the first decision was made it was easier to keep on the path of denial than to turn around.

Is this our story too? We have all abused power, whether in premeditated ways like this story or in unplanned ways. The world does not always go the way we would like it to go. At these times it is so easy to say something hurtful or become physically aggressive to someone who is smaller.

When this happens, is our response any different than David's when we are confronted by our behavior? I most often first defend. This defense usually takes on a number of different themes. One frequent defense is to blame the other person - after all if they had not pushed me I would not have responded in that way, so I can hardly be held accountable for my actions. Another frequent defense is to simply deny that I did anything inappropriate. After all it is not really my fault that the other person is so sensitive. We may even go so far as to suggest that the other person is fortunate we had the courage to tell them the truth.

What makes these defense patterns difficult to deal with is that in certain situations they are appropriate responses rather than signs of defensiveness. Another difficulty is that an interaction between two people is often complicated with one person misusing their power and the other person responding in kind. In situations like these it is difficult to identify, let alone reflect, on our behavior because all our mental energy is directed against the other person.

We also know there is an unfortunate tendency for the Bathshebas to blame themselves for power abuses inflicted on them. There is also a tendency for the Davids to defend themselves. This combination often results in these patterns continuing for extended periods of time, resulting in significant damage to both persons.

We may need to reflect to determine whether our behavior is appropriate or sinful or defensive like David's. Was I considerate of the other person's needs and feelings? Did I treat the person with respect? What would I change if I were to roll back the tape? Do I have a need to justify my actions? Did I see the other's behavior as an obstacle to meeting my wants?

Lastly, why did David not see his own reflection in Nathan's story? Nathan was wise enough to not confront David directly. He knew that David had worked hard at covering his sin; he also knew that David was a man who loved justice. So Nathan told a story. Through the story of the rich man's misuse of power, David was able to recognize himself. David could clearly see another man's abuse of power for financial gain and yet was unable to see his own abuse of power that involved the taking of a woman and the killing of her husband. How could David be so blind?

Our newspapers are filled with accusations about people's misuse of power. Rarely do we hear confessions of people who acknowledge their own abuse of power. I too, have been able to identify power plays of people around me, yet struggle with seeing and acknowledging my own power of influence. We all tend to focus on the areas where we feel powerless rather than the areas where we in turn have control, authority, or influence. Many of us spend hours accusing others of misusing their influence over our lives and yet spend little time thinking about how we can be faithful when we in turn possess the power to act or produce an effect on others.

As I prepared this sermon I realized that over the last two years other staff have talked about the amount of power I have at work. My response was to deny or minimize my power. Hiding under our Christian organization's "flat" structure, I was uncomfortable with the fact that I had power. It seemed like something unclean.

Yet I did have power, in my position, in my ability to speak clearly and in the knowledge and experience I had in the field. I still feel uncomfortable with the idea but rather than putting my energy into denying the power I do have, I am trying to be responsible with how I use that power.

This blind spot that many of us share needs to be examined. How have I used my ability to communicate clearly to keep others from expressing their views? How have you used your position in the home, work or church to get your way? How have we used our size to intimidate others, possibly even our children? Where do I have power in relationships? In exercising this power am I considering the others who will be impacted by my actions?

When I think of David's story in the light of the three questions I have explored it takes on new meaning. David's story suddenly has become my story. Why with all the women at his disposal would David even bother with Bathsheba? There are simply times in our lives, in a variety of different areas that we want more than we have or need. How could David abuse his power in this way? We all have abused the power that has been entrusted to us by those with whom we are in relationship. The greater the abuse, the greater the consequence. Why did David not repent earlier? I too have covered my tracks by using selected information to justify my decisions. I too, have taken advantage of the ones I love by knowing and using their weakness to get what I want and then talking my way out of it until I am convinced I did nothing wrong. Why did David not see his own reflection in Nathan's story? Just like David, I am much more

aware of other people's abuses of power than I am aware of my own power, let alone my misuse of it. **These** realizations are not particularly comforting.

Thank God this is not the end of the story. When David finally came to terms with what he had done, there was forgiveness. Psalm 51 which was read earlier is a moving confession. David's repentance resulted in God's forgiveness that gave David the peace and strength to deal with the future consequences. These consequences included the death of his illegitimate son and the rape of his daughter Tamar by his son Amnon. Yes, the consequences were difficult for David to bear and yet God's forgiveness was also great, for the next offspring of David and Bathsheba was Solomon. The important role that David played in the Bible is also a testimony to God's forgiveness. Even though David used his power to sexually have a woman and killed her husband to cover his misdeed, he repented and was forgiven and was subsequently known to be an ancestor, forerunner, and foreshadower of Jesus. David is a good name because of his openness to God's movement in his life and his response to his own sin.

My prayer is that we will all learn the lessons from David's story. We all have power and it is less likely to be misused if we can identify where we have it. We all struggle with using our power "with" people rather than "over" people. I pray that we will be able to choose to empower people rather than take advantage. I pray that when we fail we will have the courage to recognize our sins and repent. Let us never forget that not only does God want to forgive us, God also wants to bless us.

MAMA KADI

Be One Just as Christ is One With the Father

John 17:20-26

In our everyday lives we have the habit of saying good-bye to our friends when we want to go our separate ways whether for a short time or a long time. When Jesus felt his death approaching, he informed his disciples of what would happen to him. After hearing that their Master would die, the disciples were very discouraged. Their worry led them to think about what would happen to them in the coming absence of their Master. Jesus, knowing their thoughts, told them the following in John 14:1 *"Don't let your hearts be troubled. Believe in God, believe also in Me."* Jesus wanted his disciples to have peace. He asked them not to worry and pushed them to keep their eyes on both the Father and himself. He exhorted them to have a faith in God that was both firm and mature. God was not simply to be their God when everything seemed to go well but also and especially when they experienced the dark days of life.

After Jesus spoke to his disciples and told them everything he could about his Father, he went to pray. In John 17, Jesus prayed first of all for himself, then for his disciples and then for those who would believe in him through the testimony of these disciples.

Jesus talked to his Father in the disciples' presence. It is in this prayer that Jesus lets us see deep into his heart. His heart is full of love for those the Father has given him. It is for this reason that the prayer is called "The High Priestly Prayer." Here we see the prayer of the Great High Priest of all humanity - a prayer which begins his sacrifice by offering himself to God along with all his people, both present and future.

Jesus' prayer consists of both past realities and future events. Let's return to the past realities. In the first part of the prayer, Jesus considers his mission to be complete but he includes his approaching Passion and asks that the glory he has with the Father before the creation of the world be given back to him. When Jesus prays for himself, it is not his own person he has in mind, but rather the work of God. By asking his Father to glorify him, Jesus tell us that his glory contributes to the glory of God. The essential goal of the Son of God is the gift of eternal life defined by these words in verse 3, *"So, that they may know You, the only true God, and also know the One you have sent, your son Jesus Christ."*

Jesus had prepared and educated the 12 minus Judas whom he calls the son of perdition. In verse 12 he says that he has kept and preserved them. This is the work he has completed.

Therefore Jesus affirms the security he guaranteed to his disciples, the word that he gave them. When Jesus prays for them he asks the Father to keep them in his name so they may be one just as he himself is one with the Father. By recommending the disciples to God, Jesus sees them as continuing agents of this work. His own part of the work he sees as finished. By revealing himself as the Son, Jesus also revealed the Father that sent him.

Let us now look at the events to come!

Jesus' prayer in verses 20-26 is enlarged to include those who will come to faith through the disciples' ministry. These believers are to be "one" just as Jesus is one with the Father.

The model of unity that Jesus recommends for Christians is the unity of the Father and Son. The only way that it can be maintained is by remaining in both the Father and the Son. In other words, "As the Father lives in the Son and the Son in the Father even so the Son lives in believers and in living in them, he unites them one to the other." In this prayer Jesus points out clearly that complete unity must be manifested to the eyes of the world so the world will truly be able to discover the origin of this unity.

Jesus, by praying in the presence of his disciples wanted to show them that his bond with his Father was one of mutual love and knowledge and a common activity and possession of all things. One cannot see the Father without seeing the Son. By this prayer the disciples saw both the love and the nature of his Father - he is Holy and demands that his disciples be holy as well.

During his lifetime Jesus had the habit of withdrawing in order to be alone with his Father. It was in this way that he learned to know both his Father and his Father's will.

In this prayer Jesus undertook the ministry of intercession for the apostles but he also included all believers of all times and all places. Some of you may be asking, "What is intercession?" This noun comes from the verb "intercede" which means to place oneself between God and an individual. The intercessor more or less disappears. Instead of being involved for oneself, it's for another that the intercessor prays.

In Exodus 34:30-33 & 17:8-13, we have the story of Moses who was an intercessor for his people. Nehemiah is another example in his prayer for the rebuilding of the wall of Jerusalem. When he got there, there were people who tried to discourage him and make him afraid. But Nehemiah prayed for his enemies (Neh. 6:14). When we talk to God in prayer, he reveals himself to us as a loving and holy God; a God who involves us in the ministry of intercession for other believers and for the world. This kind of prayer is the basis of our spiritual growth. It is through prayer that we are united with Christ and through him with God and finally with each other. But often our flesh, our egotistical and proud, sinful nature, our constant search for self interest and self glorification, is the principle obstacle to God's activity in the world, particularly in Zaire.

In this prayer Jesus prays for his disciples and for those of us who come after them. How does Christian unity manifest itself in our lives? How much time do you take to pray? For whom do you pray? For Christians who are persecuted? For your brothers and sisters who are sick? For those who are in bondage to Satan? For the state and church authorities who mistreat the people God gave them to govern? Do you pray for those who are hungry? Their meal is divided in days. Today, if the children eat, the parents will go to bed hungry. And tomorrow the parents will have their turn to eat and the children will go hungry.

But do the children respect this? How will this prayer become a more concrete reality for you? Are your prayers mission-minded? Take note that prayer is a strong weapon for us as believers. By it we can fight against the schemes of the devil (Eph. 6:10-20).

Christian unity in our lives should be a unity of love, of sharing the Word of God with others, of sharing one's possessions with those who are in need. The word "sharing" is well understood among the African people for the African man never eats alone what his wife has prepared for the family. There are always the needy and strangers who benefit as well.

As Christians we must not follow the example of the Corinthian believers who were full of divisions. Some said they were followers of Apollos, others of Paul. In 1 Corinthians 3:3-9 Paul tells them that they are carnal since there is jealousy and discord among them. These Christians were living in a worldly manner. When one said "I am of Paul!" and another said "I am of Apollos", they were not united. Now the Word of God tells us that Paul and Apollos are nothing. Both are servants. If one does this work and another accomplishes another task, the two are really one. Each will receive his own reward from the Savior according to his own work. For both of them are God's workers.

At the present time the church seems to be racing toward power, and is becoming a church of separation, a church of hate and a church of a single tribe. Christians are lacking in love toward one another, lacking in knowledge of the Word of God and the sharing of their wealth. The unity demonstrated by Christ is no longer evident and the difference between believer and non believer is not really noticed.

But Jesus prayed for us that we would be one. Amen !

EVELYN LABUN

Patience - A Fruit of the Spirit

Galatians 5:22-25

I have been told by friends that I am well suited to speak on patience since I am a patient person. But the patience the writer is speaking of in Galations 5 is not a natural endowment. It is a fruit of the Spirit. It is not inborn or personality. It is a harvest or maturation of a product or quality over time because of the Spirit's work and a willingness of the person to learn from the Spirit of God. People with natural patience may find this a hard gift to cultivate since they don't know their own difficulty in developing the patience spoken of here.

The fruit of the Spirit is not legislated or commanded by God. They are attributes or attitudes that are invoked or are a natural expression of the work of the Spirit in our lives. What this means is that we have to let Christ, through the work of the Holy Spirit, rule our impatience as we personally experience it. We need to have an experience of impatience and at that point allow the work of the Spirit to enter our lives.

CLARE ANNE RUTH-HEFFELBOWER

When Someone Else Sins

Matthew 18:15-20

I've been reading *Calvin and Hobbes* cartoons again. There was one recently where Calvin is standing behind a box with "Life 5¢" written on the front. Susie walks up and says, "All right, here's a nickel. What do I get?"

Calvin, nickel in hand says, "Nothing. I just ripped you off."

"What?!" shrieks Susie.

"That's life!" replies Calvin.

The last frame shows the box smashed and the sounds of a fight going on.

Calvin and Susie act out a fantasy that probably all of us have from time to time. Someone takes advantage of me, hurts me, does me in — and I get even with them. Or at least I "make things right," then let others know I've been wronged and who did it.

Usually we're a little more civilized than these six year olds. We use the legal system to straighten things out. But we try to make sure we get what's coming to us — and so do our opponents.

Or sometimes we work at getting revenge on our own. Although nice people like us usually work at doing it in a "nice" way — which some call passive aggressive. We just nicely and sweetly and behind someone's back do something that we know will hurt them.

The end result of dealing with conflict in this way is usually some kind of distance from those who hurt us. We just don't have anything to do with them anymore. Sometimes that's the first and only thing that happens. You hurt me and you don't exist anymore as far as I'm concerned. I don't have to see you. I don't have to talk to you. And if I do, we'll keep it very formal and polite.

As we all know, these aren't necessarily the healthiest ways to deal with conflict. Jesus gives us some other guidelines for handling conflict and enemies. In the passage we just read from Matthew, he gives specific directions for dealing with conflict among Christians. It is often referred to as the Matthew 18 pattern and consists of three steps.

First, if a fellow Christian wrongs you or sins against you — some early manuscripts don't even have the "against you" phrase, just "sins" — you go to them in private and talk about it. If reconciliation comes at that stage, great! You've regained a brother or sister.

If it doesn't work, go on to step two. Take one or two other people along to talk with the offender again. This comes from the Old Testament teaching that in any dispute a person couldn't be convicted on the basis of one person's complaint. Two or three witnesses were required (Deut. 19:15). So you take a few other people along to try to talk things through.

If this doesn't work, then Matthew says, report it to the church. Make it a matter of public knowledge and let the church deal with it. If reconciliation still can't be brought about, then treat the offender like an unbeliever or tax collector. Disconnect!

This procedure has been followed by the church at times with varying results, often not very good ones. The process of excommunication developed out of this teaching. The practice of shunning or avoiding someone who is seen as disobeying the church's teaching has its roots here. Groups that have strict rules have tended to be the ones who disconnect from those who question the rules. Stories we hear about this kind of thing usually involve great pain on the part of the one being excommunicated or shunned. The problem has been that one can easily get sidetracked from the intent of Jesus' teaching here and end up becoming excessively judgmental and punitive.

Jesus is not describing this process to show us how to punish someone. He is not describing a process aimed at making sure that we get heard and our rights are respected. The main purpose of this teaching is not even to show us how to resolve disputes, although we can learn some things about that here. What Jesus is concerned about is maintaining and restoring relationships between brothers and sisters in God's family and between people and God.

The entire chapter is talking about relationships in the church. The parable of the lost sheep is placed just before the passage we read today. "What would you do," Jesus asks, "if you had a hundred sheep and one of them wandered off? Wouldn't you leave the ninety-nine on the hillside and look for the one that had wandered away?" Jesus goes on to say that God doesn't want anyone to be lost from the flock.

Then comes the teaching that we are focusing on today. Jesus recognizes how one person's wrongdoing tends to separate him or her from the flock. And he points out that it is the responsibility of the rest of the family to find them and bring them back.

Often when people are having trouble holding their lives together or when they are unable to follow Jesus faithfully, they do go away. Most churches wouldn't even have the chance to excommunicate or shun them if they wanted to — they have already left. But that leaves us in exactly the position of the shepherd with 99 sheep on the hillside and one that wandered off. It is up to us to work at finding the lost sheep and restoring the broken relationships.

What Jesus is talking about here is like a family trying to do everything within its power to help a member who is struggling. We hear heroic stories of a brother or sister giving a kidney to a sibling who needs a kidney transplant. There are families where one member struggles with insecurities, fears, handicaps, or learning disabilities and the rest of the family hangs in there trying to get whatever kind of special help is necessary. This is what Jesus is talking about. Hanging in there with people who are hurting and pulling away from the family of God.

Now if we are going to try to do that which Jesus has told us to do, it calls for some special attitudes on our part.

First of all, we need to care enough about others to want to draw them back in. This may be hard. Sometimes people who have difficulty and pull away are people who aren't very much fun to be around. Their problems are real. Caring enough about others to want to restore relationships is especially difficult if they have hurt us along the way.

If we do genuinely care about others in this way though, we have made a major step towards being able to approach them out of love and concern; the only way there can be any hope of reconciliation. This can be harder than we think because we can say the words of love and concern but the feelings that really motivate us often tend more toward self-righteousness or anger. Self-righteousness allows us to operate from a position above the muck. It highlights the person's sin for us and makes us want to do something to help them, while blinding us to our own sins or our own role in the problem. Anger is often connected to a need we have to see someone corrected. We want to make them realize how much they have hurt someone, or make them pay in some way. Although we usually don't allow ourselves to think in those terms, those motivations are often still there.

The only way we can avoid getting caught by some of these traps is to live with an ongoing sense of humility and a clear awareness of our own weakness and sin. We also need to remember that we are forgiven and we depend on God in all of our living. Along with all this, we need a willingness to forgive and the ability to own our part in a conflict and to let go of the hurt that has been done to us by someone else.

Now with all of this, we may tend to say "I can't do this. It's beyond me. I'm too imperfect to deal with anyone else's imperfections unless it has to do with hurting them back. No one but God can judge. So I'll just stay out of it." That is what many Christians and churches in today's world have tended to do.

But that is not what Jesus tells us to do. He tells us to go out and look for that lost sheep. We are to do whatever we can to avoid losing a brother or sister from the family of God. Jesus calls us to do what we can to help people be healthy, whole people who have healthy relationships in the family of God.

It may sound impossible. But it's not, as long as we allow Jesus to help us with the process. The famous promise from verse 20, *"Whenever two or three of you come together in my name, I am there with you,"* was given specifically for this situation we are talking about today. It is not just a general promise about Christ's presence in worship or small group gatherings - although Jesus is present there too. What Jesus is talking about here is that when we as brothers and sisters take on the difficult task of reaching out to someone who is pulling away, someone who has hurt others and is probably hurting themselves, Jesus is there, empowering us in a special way. Jesus is there to help with our attitudes, to help us be caring people, to help us be humble people.

With Jesus' help miraculous things can happen. The lost sheep can be found, people within the family of God can have healthy and whole relationships. Jesus calls us to be here for each other.

MERRILL UNGER

To Choose This Way

God sometimes gives us mountaintop experiences to call us back to
Faithfulness or to confirm our following.
    A particularly faithful person crosses our path.
    We are shown a vision of what can be.
    We are challenged by the biblical story.
    We see a loving and caring community.
    We are awed by the beauty of nature.
And from the mountain the words of Elijah come to us again.
"How long will you go limping between two opinions? If the Lord
is God, follow him; but if Baal, then follow him." (I Kings 18:21
NRSV)

To choose this way is to choose:
Profit of a lasting kind
A life of risk and fulfillment
Life through sacrifice
Power to live faithfully
    Working toward love in all our relationships
    Desiring peace and justice in all of life
    Finding freedom by living authentically
Confidence for the future.

P. KARUNA SHRI JOEL

Do This One Thing

Mark 16:15, 13:10 • Matthew 28:20

When I think of Christian preaching today, I am often disturbed because most of our preaching is done within the four walls of the church. Some of us hear message after message and continue in our monotonous spiritual life. We fail to react with commitment to the call of God.

Already 2000 years have gone by since Jesus told us to do this one thing. And it still remains fresh, because we have not yet done it. Jesus was very clear and powerful when he said, "Go into all the world and preach the gospel to all creation" (Mk. 6:15). This is the most important task Jesus left for his church to do. Are we doing it at all? How are we doing it? What are we doing? There are millions of people who do not know the love of Jesus. According to statistics there are still more than 2000 tribes without the gospel. Among these more than 50% do not even have the Scriptures in their language. Yet the commission of Jesus Christ is clear that the universe must be evangelized. It pricks my heart when I think of God who sent his only Son Jesus Christ. Are we today encouraging and sending our children to be missionaries or to be mere professionals? What are we aiming at in our teaching and preaching? More than 60% of the people in our universe have yet to be reached. We can no longer keep quiet given this terrible fact. Could we not do something? How can we respond to this great Commission?

Decide to become a disciple of Jesus Christ.

Jesus plainly explains the cost of discipleship in Mark 8:34, *"If anyone would come after me he must deny himself and take up his cross and follow me."* The word "if" is an open invitation, there is no force in Jesus' gentle call. "If anyone" also shows the importance of each one's decision.

When Jesus calls us and gives us an option to choose, he calls us with a definite purpose and gives us assurance. Therefore the call of God inspires us to decide. The prophet Isaiah, in spite of his inability, decided to go when he felt the touch of God and said, "Here am I. Send me." (Is. 6:7,8) Our God is a God of the possible and therefore our response should be positive. The second step is denying and emptying oneself. Denying oneself is the starting point of the cost of discipleship. As we "take up the cross and follow" we will be guided through.

Jesus chose disciples who were young and energetic. They had enthusiasm and accepted the challenge to give their lives. Today, some of the young and energetic are very insensitive and do not respond to Jesus' call.

I am one of the products of missionary work here in India. The place where I was born, brought up and am living at presently is called the "Mission Compound." If no missionaries had came to India over one hundred years ago, I would have been born into a different situation altogether. I would not have been what I am now. To put it briefly, I became a Christian, because I believed; I believed because I heard. I heard because someone preached; someone preached because they decided to come to India with the gospel of Jesus Christ. Therefore God gives us similar responsibilities. It was the strong convictions of the missionary workers which led me to become a full-time minister. And likewise today there are many people whose duty it is to carry on the task.

Dear brothers and sisters, we have the message of life. Don't withhold it from those who need it. Let us decide to go out and reach those who have never heard. When you decide and are sure of your call and commitment the next step is:

Preach the gospel

There is only one important thing which the Lord Jesus Christ has entrusted to us, that is to preach and evangelize the whole world. Jesus introduced us to the mission field here on earth. His mission field is the whole world (whole creation). The task that is given to us now is to preach the word of God. "Preaching" is one of the privileges given by God to his followers and disciples. The word "preach" means "to declare and to proclaim" the good news. Even Jesus' own message and mission was to preach the

good news. The good news is that salvation comes through Christ Jesus the Lord. The Apostle Paul clearly cautions in II Corinthians 4:5 *"We do not preach ourselves, but Jesus Christ as Lord."* And it is done with authority. Preaching is not done in isolation. *"You shall receive power when the Holy Spirit has come on you"* (Acts 1: 8). Therefore the Holy Spirit is the authority and power behind our preaching. There is power in the gospel to evangelize the world (Rom. 1:16). And the presence of God will be with us when we go out to preach, as it is promised by Jesus in Matthew 28:20.

Now, the question is, what is happening to Christian preaching today? Are we preaching Christ our Lord? The Apostle Paul was a powerful and successful missionary who traveled around with the gospel and faced hardships, persecutions, and imprisonment. Yet he writes to Timothy his spiritual son, *"Preach the Word; be prepared in season and out of season"* (II Tim.4:2). Paul's vision and mission was evangelism. What is our vision and what is our mission? The final commission of Jesus Christ is an ongoing program. Therefore we must teach and train others.

Make disciples of Christ

Jesus trained 12 young men and then the 70 so in turn they could train other people to carry on the work. Paul had many converts, but he ordained elders and encouraged many people to carry on the task. Wherever he went, he not only preached, he also taught or trained. Our vision needs to be broadened and extended. We can not confine our mission to the four walls of the church, we need to reach the outside world and train others to go out to reach the unreached. This was exactly what Jesus intended. He trained and sent his disciples out to the world. Now we need to follow his method and encourage young people to commit their lives for this great task. Our young people need to be trained to become evangelists and teachers according to their gifts and be sent out to preach the good news to the entire world. As Paul says it, we are *"teaching everyone in all wisdom, so that we may present everyone mature in Christ"* (Col. 1:28). NRSV

Now, my dear brothers and sisters, are you not ready to decide to become the disciples of Christ? Don't you feel sensitive to this great commission of Christ? How long can you sit back, remain aloof and uninvolved in Christ's mission?

Are you willing to respond to this glorious task? If you are open and sensitive to his call, you would surely decide. Once you decide, you will definitely follow him, become a missionary and be part of this meaningful task.

There are three categories of people here, young, middle aged, and older adults. All of us can become part of this task.

Recently when I attended a revival meeting, one of the songs touched my heart more powerfully than the sermon. The meaning of the song goes like this:

There are many in the world who
do not know my name,
There are very few to carry the
gospel to them.
Can any one of you decide to go
to them and tell them of my love?
Can any one? At least one of you?
If you can not go, can you send
someone who is willing to go?
Can you support someone to go?
Can you at least pray for these
people to be reached some day?

My dear brothers and sisters, I would repeat the same thing. Where do you stand? Are you not touched? Can you go and tell others of God's love?

May the Lord touch you and lead you through.

This may be Karuna's last sermon. It was written expressly for this collection. Karuna and her eight month old daughter Sneha died on July 7, 1996 as a result of a motor accident. She was at age 32 a spiritual giant. On less than one day's notice over 2000 people came to her funeral. A thanksgiving memorial service was held for them on Augsut 3 and over 1000 people came to give thanks for her influence and for how she had impacted their lives. Karuna will be remembered as a woman who made a difference in the kingdom of God.

Elsie Ann Kroeker, an MBMS Mission Associate in India along with her husband, Werner, was instrumental in obtaining and submitting Karuna's sermon, testimony and picture. Of Karuna's death, she writes, "The loss to the MB conference in India is beyond comprehension. And to us too."

NADINE PENCE FRANTZ

All of Us Are Witnesses

Acts 2:1-24, 32-47 NRSV

All of us are witnesses.

All of us are witnesses to the many changes and movements of God in the world around us. When future generations ask us about the opening of the Eastern block, we will be able to tell them the story of how the borders were opened and how the Wall came down. When they ask how our perception of the Soviet Union changed from that of the "Evil Empire" to that where the Soviet president could walk down a Washington D.C. street shaking hands, we will be able to tell them stories of politics and *perestroika*. When they ask us about the beginning of the end of apartheid in South Africa, we can tell them the story of Nelson Mandela and President De Klerk.

All of us are witnesses to the many movements of the Spirit around us.

The book of Acts tells us how faithful, devout Jews were coming to the city of Jerusalem for the festival of Pentecost. They came from every nation, to celebrate the Festival of Weeks which marks the fiftieth day after Passover and the harvest of the first fruits of the season. They came upon a house where the followers of the one who called himself Jesus of Nazareth were staying and heard from inside the house strange, bewildering things. There were a multitude of languages being spoken and yet the ones inside were all Galileans. They were speaking about God's power and deeds and yet the one they called the Christ had been killed 40 days before. "They are filled with new wine," was the comment, "there can be no other explanation."

"It is all politics," we say, "nothing could really change South African apartheid that quickly."

I held out for a long time in disbelief, assuming there would be little change in South Africa despite what President De Klerk said. I was one of the cynics watching the release of the political prisoners, thinking they would never dare release Mandela. And even with his release, I didn't believe he would be taken seriously. "It's all superficial," I said, "the South African government could never seriously consider a change so radical and so deep." But I and the other skeptics were wrong. Politics or not, the changes have started. Politics or not, the anti-apartheid groups are meeting with the government groups to talk about the economy. New wine or not, the disciples are proclaiming that Jesus is risen, that he is not dead. Not drunk, but filled with ecstatic excitement, the followers of Jesus are proclaiming that it is indeed Jesus who is the expected Messiah.

All of us are witnesses to the change and movement and presence of the Spirit around us. All of us are witnesses to the surprising ways in which God moves and acts. Who could have anticipated such things? Who could have plotted them out? Who could know where the wind will blow next?

David and I struggled for years to have children. We went through tests, procedures, more tests, and medications. We were on quite a medical regimen to see if we could have a child. Emotionally exhausted, we took a break from it all, to see what was ahead, to see if we wanted to go on with any more medical options. Then, out of the blue, there came a call from a friend in Bakersfield. "Did we want to adopt a child? Did we want to adopt a child that would be born in six months to a young high school girl who had decided she could not raise it?" In six months, we held Bryan and we became parents, not as we expected, not as we had planned and calculated, but fully and truly parents, none the less.

God does come. God does act. That is Peter's sermon to the crowd at Pentecost. "Fellow Israelites," he says, "let the entire house of Israel know with certainty that God has made Jesus both Lord and Messiah. God has raised from the dead the one who was crucified. Jesus is the long-awaited Messiah, the one who will bring all our enemies to our feet, the one who will bring about the reign of God. Listen, all you faithful and devout people. The reign of God is not coming in the way that you expect. The reign of God is coming through the one named Jesus who is the Christ. And the promise is for you, for your children, and for all who are far away, everyone whom the Lord our God calls to him" (Acts 2:32-39, paraphrase).

God does come. God does act. But most likely not in the way we expect, not in the ways we predict. Whenever we gather together for communion, whenever we take the bread and the cup, we anticipate, as a body, the presence of God in and among us. Coming together at the table of the Lord is our way of opening ourselves to the presence of the Spirit and to its movement in our lives. But we do not know how that will be manifested. We do not know how we will be touched as a body. Who we are and how we are God's is in God's hands. We are but witnesses of all that takes place. We are only able to watch it, experience it, and proclaim it. We do not bring it about.

As the United States of America we have set ourselves up as the protector of democracy, as the deliverer of freedom to the world. We have planned carefully how to bring that about; we have calculated our resources and our might and have invested it in countries we thought had a chance of moving towards democracy, countries that would respond to our help with a shift in the balance of power. And while we have been tinkering and plotting in Central America, in another corner of the world the Berlin Wall comes down, and the Eastern borders are open. While we are miscalculating the devastating effect of our actions in the Iran-Contra affair, the Spirit blows elsewhere and the power of God changes the shape of the world we live in.

God does act. God does come. Whether we're there or not. Whether we are inside the house receiving the tongues of fire or whether we are outside watching it happen. There are times when all we can do is repent; there are times when all we can do is bow before the almighty presence of God and repent of our past actions that have been against God's presence and God's spirit, repent of our actions which have hindered the Spirit, and be baptized into the new reality that is before us. Most likely, we will find ourselves receiving the good news in unanticipated ways rather than our calculated ways. God moves and acts and sometimes we are but witnesses.

But then we are given the power of witnessing to others of the mighty acts we have seen. Then we are asked to repent and believe and proclaim that what we have experienced is of God. The miracle of Pentecost, the birth of the church is that those who were outside heard and believed. They saw the events, heard the tongues of fire, and then were convinced by Peter that what they had seen and heard was of God. And they welcomed this message, repented, and were baptized, about three thousand of them. According to Acts 2:

> *They devoted themselves to the apostles' teaching and fellowship, to the breaking of bread and the prayers. Awe came upon everyone, because many wonders and signs were being done by the apostles. All who believed were together and had all things in common; they would sell their possessions and goods and distribute the proceeds to all, as any had need. Day by day, as they spent much time together in the temple, they broke bread at home and ate their food with glad and generous hearts, praising God and having the goodwill of all the people." (42-47a)*

That was the miracle of Pentecost—that so many who had anticipated God would come to them in the form of a King, as a new David, now were touched by God and believed he had come in the form of the crucified and resurrected Christ, the one they had known as Jesus.

All of us are witnesses. We are witnesses to the many events around us which demonstrate the movement and action of God in our lives. We are witnesses to the surprising, new beginnings which the Spirit brings to our lives, which require us to repent, to change our ways, and to follow one we previously thought was of no account. And all of us are witnesses as our lives and our words proclaim what it means to follow the one whom we call Christ, follow the one we knew as Jesus, the one who died and was then resurrected. May our lives reflect that change in direction, that new power, that following after the Jesus who calls us.

Amen.

Cover Art Interpretation

Pentecost 1990

This painting was created by Janice Leppke as a visual reaction to a sermon delivered by Dena Pence Frantz in 1990. The content of the sermon dealt with God's intervention in the events of the world just preceding the date of the sermon. The radically changing politics of South Africa and the Soviet Union along with the fall of the Berlin Wall were given as examples of how God works to create new pentecosts in times and places where hope for change might have been lost or unexpected.

"God does come. God does act. But most likely not in the way we expect, not in the ways we predict. . . We are but witnesses of all that takes place. We are only able to watch it, experience it, and proclaim it. We do not bring it about." (Pence Frantz, 1990)

Janice says of her painting, "It came to me while Dena was preaching and I immediately sketched it and then went home and began painting. To me sermons are never complete without a response factor. This piece was painted to be a religious piece." When the painting was completed and hung in the sanctuary where it was given birth, one of the men said, "We didn't need a sermon, the painting itself was enough of a sermon." *Pentecost 1990* has enhanced the worship in many services at the College Community Mennonite Brethren Church in Clovis, CA. The original painting is currently on display at the Mennonite Brethren Biblical Seminary in Fresno, CA. The repeated black and white images of *Pentecost 1990* used throughout the book are a symbol of our varying responses to the spoken word of God.

Janice Leppke has been painting seriously for ten years using water color as her primary medium. Her work is exhibited at various places in Fresno, including the Door Art Gallery. She is a member of College Community M.B. Church in Clovis, CA. Janice and her husband, Ken, have three daughters. For the past six years she has been adjunct faculty in the Teacher Education Department and the Art Department at Fresno Pacific College. Recently she began working for the Mennonite Central Committee out of the West Coast office as Resource Developments Coordinator.

Testimony

P. Karuna Shri Joel

I am P. Karuna Shri Joel, married, mother of three children, working as a full time minister in the MB Conference in India.

I was born to God-fearing Mennonite Brethren parents in India, on the 8th of February, 1964 in Wanaparthy. My father, S.S. Krupiah and my mother, B.D. Kanthamma have taught in the MB high schools in India for 30 years.

When I was doing my 12th standard I thought to myself that I should go to Bible School and learn the Word of God. It was mere interest that led me to Bible School. As I was doing my pre-theology at MB Bible School, Shamshabad, I realized some strong force within myself encouraging me to go for further Biblical studies. One day God spoke to me and said, "even though you never thought that you would continue in Biblical training, it is Me who is calling you to full-time ministry." This inner force clearly led me to commit myself into the mighty hands of God and dedicate my life to him.

Saying 'yes' to God often means saying 'good-bye' to many things of this world. There-fore I decided along with my parents' consent to pursue further theological training in order to equip myself for God's ministry.

At the age of 21 I was married to P. Menno Joel, a servant of God, on May 20, 1985 at my home town. I would call my marriage a "miracle." The interesting part of my marriage was that it was arranged without any knowledge on my part. It's not strange in India to have arranged marriages without the consent of the girl. Another interesting thing was that the person whom I married was my teacher in my pre-theology course at Shamshabad. My first reaction to this proposal was, "No, he was my teacher and he must be much older than me, how am I going to get married to this man?" My father replied, "You probably did not pray for this man thus far, but you know I have been praying for this man for one year, and miraculously this proposal came from his parents." Then I immediately said "yes" to this. I was surprised and realized the promise, that you did not choose this man, but I chose to give him to you, to share your life together. And certainly I would say that it is perfectly God's will for my life for me to have this wonderful husband.

I am grateful to God for this miraculous will of God, and I am always thankful for the wonderful life partner with whom I am sharing not only my life but God's ministry together. Praise the Lord! I was able to do most of my theological studies after my marrage. My family and children were never a hindrance to my studies; this was a true blessing from God to me. This is not common with many married Indian women.

One of the strongest reasons leading me to go for higher theological studies was that there are very few women in the MB Church in India who have done theological studies. Therefore I thought I should go for further studies to equip myself better to motivate young men and women to study. There is a great need in the Church today to study the Word of God, and a quest for a deeper theological understanding of the Word.

Another important reason for doing further studies was my experience with different aspects of the role of women in the Church. In my opinion there is an urgent need for a radical rethinking of the Church's theology and biblical understanding in relation to women. Therefore I feel it is essential to have theologically trained women in the church who have an awareness of their potential and value as individuals. Furthermore this awareness can be developed by exposing the ideas in the programs and policies of the church by women's active and responsible participation.

The Indian culture, though it respects women in general, in some of its cultural norms and practices does not accept women who expose their talents and gifts. And even in the church today there is a lot of discrimination between men and women and their participation.

This was a burning desire in my mind, and I was seeking an answer for the role of women from the scriptures. Theological training also helped me to understand this issue. To understand church structures we need to go back into history. In the early church it was not a taboo for women to hold offices in the worshipping congregations. Jesus Christ, the person on whom the church was founded, did not regard women as inferior. We don't find any reference or suggestion in the Gospels to that effect. On the other hand we find Jesus giving important responsibilities to women, defying all existing social norms. Along with the 12 apostles he had a group of women who followed him. Women were also entrusted with the task of communicating the message of the resurrection. Even in the early church, in the times of Paul, there were women leaders. But as church organizations evolved into established forms, the existing customs of the society were absorbed into the church.

In my theological studies, I specialized in homiletics. Here again, this was a challenging decision. In the MB churches in India, preaching done by women is not accepted. But I still hope the day will come. Right now I can at least teach students how to preach through Homiletics and other related Christian Ministry subjects at the Mennonite Brethren Centenary Bible College in Shamsabad. This is the fulfillment of my desire.

The theme of my thesis was *An Assessment of Lay Involvement in the Preaching in Selected Congregations of Mennonite Brethren Churches in Andhra Pradesh*. The reason for choosing this topic was that the role of laity in the church has become a universal phenomena. The laity's participation in the ministry of preaching is a significant move towards the total task of the church. And lay involvement in the ministry of preaching is one of the contemporary issues of the Mennonite Brethren Churches in Andhra Pradesh. This issue needs to be answered in the light of exegetic principles and through empirical study.

I completed my Bachelor of Theology course in South India Biblical Seminary, Bangarapet, Bangalore from 1982-1984. I did my Bachelor of Divinity course at Andhra Christian Theological College, Hyderabad from 1987-1990. From 1992 -1994 I completed my Masters Degree at United Theological College, Bangalore, India.

My desire and dream for Indian women is that I will be able to encourage them to explore their talents and gifts and also provide a basic perception of the status and role of women in India. I would like to tell them that "you are okay to be a woman and you are precious in the sight of God."

Secondly, through my ministry with women I hope to develop a clear understanding of the biblical experiences and message for women. I also want to equip women with basic skills in analyzing the dynamics of social processes and provide a working knowledge of basic principles and practices.

Thirdly, I would like to enable women to find training designs that are relevant and applicable to their own situations. I believe in mutual submission and love. Therefore I would like to encourage both men and women to come out of their shells!

I believe and hope that the Indian women, particularly Mennonite Brethren women, will very soon find the way to exercise their equality and their talents for the extension of God's kingdom.

Presently, I am working as an executive secretary for the Mennonite Brethren Women's Conference in India. This involves working closely with the various women's groups in the churches, encouraging women to develop their leadership qualities and talents for the ministry of God. In the villages we are trying to motivate women to come out of their ignorance and superstitions. We are doing this through seminars, workshops, conferences, retreats, etc. This is a challenging ministry in which to be involved.

I am also currently involved in literature ministry. We have a monthly magazine called *Suvarthamani*, the official spiritual magazine of the MB Conference of India. A few months ago I was appointed chief editor for this magazine. For this I write articles for women and children along with other editing responsibilities. The purpose of having the magazine is to nurture men, women, youth, and children through spiritual insights and truths. We have over 1000 subscribers since 1988.

These responsibilities allow me to do a lot of thinking, writing, traveling and participating in meetings which sometimes result in criticism, tensions, and also compliments. Above all God's continuous grace sustains me to bear everything and anything. I am a small vessel in his mighty hands.

Written three months prior to her death.

Scriptural Index

Contributors

Ruth Buxman
An environmentally conscious farmer; formerly a pastor in San Francisco and a chaplain at Dallas, OR Care Center; occasional preacher; an MDiv graduate of MBBS.

Lorraine Dick
Associate pastor of Christian Education at South Langley MB church in BC; her most delightful church involvement is working through spiritual growth issues with children; author of a discipleship program for children.

Selma Enns
A full-time minister of visitation in the Kitchener, ON. MB Church which involves prison ministry; helps lead several Bible study groups; serves on various committees in the church and broader Mennonite community.

Connie Epp
A music teacher involved in worship planning and leading; involved in the diaconate and preaching in her local church; part of the Faith and Life Committee on the provincial level; currently studying theology and drama.

Irma Epp
A retired school teacher and former missionary in Zaire; involved in worship leadership and speaking in home, church, and at ladies groups and retreats; has served as assistant pastor and several interim pastoral positions in local church; vice-chair of the Mennonite Brethren Biblical Seminary board.

Nancy Riediger Fehderau
A creative church worker involved in visual aids for worship, storytelling workshops, dramatic readings and a weekly study group for young Moms; involved in various committees locally and provincially; spent many years in missionary translation work in Zaire and Kenya.

Nadine Pence Frantz
Associate Professor of Theology at Bethany Theological Seminary, IN; former pastor of an MB church in California and a visiting Assistant Professor of Theology at MBBS.

Delores Friesen
Associate Professor of Pastoral Counseling and Director of Marriage, Family and Child Counseling Program at MBBS; involved in preaching and teaching in home congregation and beyond; missionary in West Africa for 13 years; author of two previous books.

Nadine Friesen
A full-time pastor in Hillsboro, KS responsible for discipleship ministries for children and adults, women's ministries, special events and festivities; enjoys reading, spending time with friends and family, and Bible teaching.

Tiffany Friesen
A high school mathematics teacher; involved in worship leadership, youth ministry and small group leadership.

Carley Friesen-Blank
A minister in a Presbyterian church in Oregon; a former instructor in Biblical Studies at Fresno Pacific College and Tabor College; an M. Div. graduate from Fuller Theological Seminary.

Gertrud Geddert

Served on a pastoral team in Germany; teaches a Bible Survey course at Mennonite Brethren Biblical Seminary; preaches occasionally in her home church.

Mary Anne Isaak

A graduate of MBBS; has served a 3-year missionary term in Zaire and a 1-year term at St. Petersborough College in Russia; hopes to pursue doctoral studies; involved in teaching, youth work and small groups in local church in Montreal, Quebec.

Jean Janzen

A poet; author of several volumes of poetry; awarded National Endowment of the Arts Award in 1996; a teacher of poetry at Fresno Pacific University; a worship leader in her home congregation.

P. Karuna Shri Joel

A former full-time minister in the MB Conference in India involved in conference-wide women's ministry, literature and worship ministry; taught homiletics at the MB Centenary Bible College in Shamshabad.

Mama Kadi

An evangelist and Director of Women's Work in Zaire; was a teacher in the Evangelical Theological School in Kinshasa; was a speaker at the 1990 Mennonite World Conference, Winnipeg, Man.

Joanne Klassen

Community Mental Health worker and private practice therapist; involved in preaching and worship leadership in home congregation; choir director and musician; graduate of MBBS with a M.A. in theology and a M.A. in Marriage, Family and Child Counselling (MFCC).

Sarah Klassen

A poet with three published collections; a retired English teacher; in her second year of teaching at Lithuania Christian College; involved with worship planning and library work in her local church; former editor of *Sophia* magazine.

Sylvia Klauser

An MBBS pastoral care graduate; interested in developing a theology for Anabaptist women that is relevant today; interested in teaching theology; serving as a pastoral intern at Clovis Community Church, CA.

Evelyn Labun

A program coordinator at a local community college; working on her Doctorate of Nursing Science; her dissertation is on the cultural discovery experience of nurses working with the Vietnamese; active in her local church in various capacities.

Janice Leppke

A watercolor painter; an educator in the Teacher Education department at Fresno Pacific University; works part time at the Mennonite Central Committee office in Reedley, CA; a partner at the Door Art Gallery, a cooperative owned by nine female artists; serves on her local church council.

Dorothy Martens

Full-time congregational pastor of Family Ministries in Sardis, BC; former public health nurse in northern Canada; MBBS graduate in Marriage, Family and Child Counseling.

Hedy Leonora Martens

A Marriage and Family therapist in Winnipeg, MB; part of an association of private therapists who share an Anabaptist faith perspective; involved in workshops and seminars on theological or relational issues.

Gudrun Matties
Has been very active in MCC women's concerns and the Ontario women's network; spent nine years in Africa with MCC; continues to have an active interest in community work; speaks occasionally at women's assemblies.

Linda Matties
A teacher and librarian in British Columbia; involved in preaching in her home congregation, presenting workshops and committee leadership; M. Div. graduate of MBBS; writer of articles, book reviews and text for the MB Study Guide.

Lori Matties
Homemaker; freelance writer; editor of *Sophia*, a magazine offering a forum for women in the Mennonite Brethren Church; a member of the Olive Branch Society, a SELFHELP craft store; has been a worship planner in various churches for a number of years.

Mary Thiessen Nation
A missionary with World Impact Inc.; Ph.D. student at Fuller Theological Seminary; a pastor's spouse; spent many years in missionary work in inner Los Angeles; has taught a course on Spirituality in Urban Mission at MBBS, AMBS and Fuller.

Barbara Nikkel
A violin and writing course teacher; had a children's novel published in 1996 and a poetry book in 1997; actively involved in home church as speaker, worship and song leader; graduate of Goshen College.

Elfrieda Nikkel
Working as a counselor with Burden Bearer's of Canada; involved in women's ministry in local church and in conjunction with her husband's ministry to encourage and start new church plants; past Dean of Women at Bethany Bible Institute, Hepburn, SK.

Elaine Pinto
Chaplain in a Winnipeg hospital; has an M. Div. in Clinical Pastoral Education; actively involved in worship leadership in local congregation; served in para church leadership for several years.

Valerie Rempel
Assistant Professor of Church History and Theology at Mennonite Brethren Biblical Seminary, Fresno, CA; a Ph.D. candidate at Vanderbilt University.

Clare Ann Ruth-Heffelbower
A pastor in Clovis CA; Conference Minister for Northern California Pacific Southwest Mennonite Conference; involved in many facets of the church; an M. Div. graduate of MBBS

Laura Schmidt Roberts
Assistant professor of Bible at Fresno Pacific University; preacher and facilitator at College Hour; does occasional preaching and teaching in local church.

Janet Schmidt
Teaching conflict resolution at Mindolo Training Center, Zambia; former mediator at Mediation Services and sessional lecturer at the University of Winnipeg; a leadership commission member in local church.

Elfrieda Schroeder
A Ph.D. student in German; teacher of Introductory German at the University of Waterloo, ON;

involved in the diaconate and as a Sunday School teacher in her local church.

Dale Taylor

Administrator for MCC Canada; past assistant professor at Concord College, Winnipeg, MB; M. Div. graduate of MBBS; enjoys music, sports, and books.

Karen Heidebrecht Thiessen

A full-time pastor in a Winnipeg MB church; M. Div. graduate of MBBS; active in provincial and wider Mennonite Brethren concerns.

Vange Willms Thiessen

Family Therapist and Educational Coordinator in BC; involved in creative worship planning in local church; involved in mediation in congregation and in community settings; former community health worker and nursing instructor; MA/MFCC graduate of MBBS.

Merrill Unger

A counselor and therapist; former chaplain at University of Brandon, MB; pastor's spouse involved in adult ministries; spent one year working with Second Stage housing for abused women; an MA/MFCC graduate of MBBS.

Shirley Unrau

In pastoral team ministry in BC; involved in leading, discipling and counseling in women's ministry; speaker at women's banquets and retreats; church pianist and sings in choir and duets.

Faith Wiebe

A 1996 MBBS M. Div. graduate in pastoral care; musician, writer; piano teacher; open to pastoral ministry.

Katie Funk Wiebe

Professor Emeritus of Tabor College; a writer of hundreds of articles and numerous books; a frequent workshop and retreat speaker; works as freelance writer and editor; serves as member on several MB boards as well as Window to the World, a SELFHELP craft shop in Wichita, KS.